Shame-Free Parenting

SANDRA D. WILSON, Ph.D.

INTERVARSITY PRESS
DOWNERS GROVE, ILLINOIS 60515

InterVarsity Press is the book-publishing division of InterVarsity Christian Fellowship, a student movement active on campus at hundreds of universities, colleges and schools of nursing in the United States of America, and a member movement of the International Fellowship of Evangelical Students. For information about local and regional activities, write Public Relations Dept, InterVarsity Christian Fellowship, 6400 Schroeder Rd, P.O. Box 7895, Madison, WI 53707-7895.

Cover photograph: Peter French

ISBN 0-8308-1625-9

Printed in the United States of America ∞

Library of Congress Cataloging-in-Publication Data

Wilson, Sandra D, 1938-
    Shame-free parenting/Sandra D. Wilson.
        p.   cm.
    Includes bibliographical references (p.   ).
    ISBN 0-8308-1625-9
    1. Parenting—United States.   2. Parents—United States—
Attitudes.   3. Parent and child—United States.   4. Parenting—
Religious aspects—Christianity.   L Title.
HQ755.83.W58   1992
649'.1—dc20   92-1656
                                                 CIP

---

17   16   15   14   13   12   11   10   9   8   7   6   5   4   3   2
05   04   03   02   01   00   99   98   97   96   95   94   93

This book is dedicated, first and above all,
to the glory of God—
the only true father I have ever known.

This book is dedicated also to Dabney Kristyne Wilson,
my only grandchild—
the first of a new generation and God's promise of a new beginning.

Many individuals helped make this book a reality:

Linda Doll, my IVP editor,
who worked with a light and loving touch;

Dr. Ray Dupont, my senior pastor, and all the staff at
Faith Evangelical Free Church,
who labored in prayer as I labored at the word processor; and

my children, Becky and Dave, who
consistently love and forgive me despite my parenting failures.

My husband, Garth, deserves special thanks for
patiently enduring many personal sacrifices as I wrote this book,
and for faithfully reaffirming his belief that
God had called me to do it.

To all these dear people, and to all the other parents and children
whose lives are woven into the fabric of this book,
I declare my profound appreciation.

Introduction

The day we drove home from the hospital with our three-day-old son, my husband turned to me as if a new thought had just struck him. His question was, "Sandy, do you know anything about raising kids?"

Both of us felt (and were) very new at this big responsibility called parenting. But my fears went further. I thought, *how will I be a good parent to this little boy when my own childhood was so painful and I turned out such a failure?*

This is a book for those of us who wonder how we got to be parents when we can't remember being children.

It is for parents trying to love our children a lot when we don't like ourselves even a little.

And this book is for those of us disappointed that our children aren't able to fill the cracks in our marriages and bring us happiness and fulfillment. (We want them to do that for us, even though we couldn't do it for our own parents, no matter how hard we tried.)

But perhaps this book's most distinctive feature is that *this is a parenting book for parents.*

Most books about parenting are written primarily for the benefit of the readers' children. Most seem to focus on our children's identity struggles, needs and feelings to resolve the major parenting problems we face. Clearly, our children's identity struggles, needs and feelings are very important. But *so are ours*—even if we don't know what they are. *Especially* if we don't know what they are! And if we don't, that probably means we were raised in an unhealthy family.

Unhealthy families are, to one degree or another, shame-bound families. Shame springs from the lie that adults are supposed to be perfect and problem-free and that children should be short, permanent-press adults. In these families, parents don't *resolve* personal or family problems, because they believe they shouldn't *have* any personal or family problems. These problem-laden parents are impaired in their capacity to provide consistently adequate parenting.

And a child in a shame-bound family tends to grow up believing that there is something uniquely flawed in him or her because the parents' unrealistic expectations are always beyond reach. That child learns to feel different from and worth less than all the (as the child imagines) perfect people in the world.

In unhealthy families we weren't taught to know and respect ourselves and we weren't prepared for adult life. We were not allowed to be children with children's legitimate needs and feelings. So now, as adults, we probably don't know what our needs and feelings are, let alone how to get them met or express them appropriately. We may feel like insecure, incompetent little kids "playing house" who discover that we are supposed to know how to be *real* parents to *real* children.

Is it any wonder we find it hard to connect with our children and their needs and feelings? Is it any wonder we usually feel overwhelmed with our parenting responsibilities and underwhelmed with our parenting capabilities? And is it any wonder we fear that, ten or twenty years from now, our *children* will be reading this book?

"What can I do to help prevent that?" you ask. We know we can't change our parents or our pasts. In fact, the only parent I can change is *my children's* parent. When I do, I help to create a new future for me, for my children and for my grandchildren. And you can do the same. As we ourselves become personally, relationally and spiritually healthier, so will our children and our families.

We know that parenting is a tough job. After all, any enterprise that begins with something called "labor" can't be easy! So, we aren't seeking easier parenting—just healthier parenting. Here's what you will find in the following pages to help you reach that goal.

First, we will examine our own shame-bound parenting styles and their roots in our parents' parenting of us. No, this is not a "parent-bashing" book. Remember, nearly all parents do the best they know. Our parents likely would have done better if they had known what "better" was.

Then we will look at the principles of shame-free parenting, and particularly at how we can choose life by choosing truth and grace.

Next, we'll face the frustrating fact of what we don't know about healthy, shame-free parenting. We'll explore and learn some of what we don't know . . . like how to teach our children to know God, accept human limitations, *like* themselves, communicate respectfully, handle emotions appropriately, set personal boundaries, have fun and be separate individuals. All that is quite a challenge when we may not have a clue about how to do any of these things.

Finally, we will focus on the life-giving legacies we bequeath to our offspring when we choose truth and grace. We will see that there really is hope!

Along the way, I include questions you can use to evaluate your parenting and to work toward positive change. I'll also be sharing some of my personal parenting struggles—both the joy of victory and the agony of defeat. And you and I are not alone. One estimate says that in the United States alone there are *nearly 150 million* adult children of dysfunctional (what I am calling shame-bound) families.[1]

Some of us adult children are parenting veterans. However, many of us seem to have accumulated more wrinkles than wisdom over the years. I spent most of my full-nest years just wearing out instead of wising up. I have had to admit my mistakes, ask for forgiveness, and cope with residual guilt and shame. It has been a difficult and painful process, yet I wish I had started it years before I did. In fact, like many of you, I regret that I didn't begin my recovering/changing process when my children were babies. But at least I began.

Believe me, *it is never too late to begin.*[2] Even though we won't control our children in the way we could when they were very young, our growing healthier will profoundly influence them toward their own growing healthier. And God, the ultimate controller/influencer, cares deeply about our relationships with our children. After all, parent-child relationships were his design. And God desires to turn the hearts of parents and children toward one another. (See Mal 4:6.)

Most important, God promises to give us wisdom when we ask him for it. (See Jas 1:5.) He says he will be with us when we are uncertain and afraid. (For just one example, see Is 41:10.) He gives us his program for changing our parenting—or anything else in our lives. (See Rom 12:2.) And God tells us that Scripture is the light we need for all our changing paths. (See Ps 119:105.) Said differently, the Bible is the all-time, ultimate, best-selling how-to-change guide-book and parenting-repair kit. So I will be referring to scriptural passages and principles throughout the following chapters.

My earlier book *Released from Shame* details the foundational con-cepts underlying this book. In appendix C, I list chapters from *Released from Shame,* along with other helpful materials, that relate to various chapters of this book.

Many people find it helpful to keep a personal journal of thoughts and feelings as they read. You can use your journal to record answers to each chapter's "Personal Reflections" questions and to note in-sights you are discovering from Scripture. Also, you may want to write out your prayers and later record the answers.

Finally, remember we have the hope that, although we may have had significantly *im*paired parents, we can give our children substan-tially *re*paired parents!

1
Shame-Bound Parenting: Roots and Fruits

I *never wanted to be a good parent.*
I never really cared about having a consistently well-functioning family. No, what I desperately desired was to be a *perfect* parent and have a *perfect* family.

These unrealistic goals sprang from the pain-soaked soil of my childhood. I never saw, spoke to, had a photo of or even a handwriting scrap from my biological father. I believed my alcoholic stepfather was my birth father until my mother told me the truth when I was ten. Mother divorced my stepfather three years later when his alcohol-induced violence escalated to a life-threatening level.

As I grew, so did my desire to create in reality the fantasy family I had dreamed about constantly as a child. I longed so much to provide for my children the stable, peaceful home life I had never known. My goal was not moderate stability and peace. No, nothing less than perfect family tranquility would suffice.

If you too have pursued those lofty parenting and family goals, then you probably can identify with the despair I felt most of my adult years whenever I would mercilessly assess myself as a parent and as a person. I didn't do that very often. It hurt too much!

Why do we keep expecting to be perfect people and perfect parents when we regularly fail to be either? And why do we feel like such a disappointment to our parents, our children and ourselves? I think we will understand the answers to these disquieting questions when we understand the devastating lie of *shame*.

The Lie of Shame

Shame is a soul-deep sense that *there is something uniquely wrong with me* that is not wrong with you or anyone else in the world. Because I am not perfect and problem-free, I feel hopelessly, disgustingly different and worth less than other people. I view myself as, literally, worthless. It isn't just that I *make* a mistake when I make a mistake; I *am* a mistake when I make a mistake. This is shame's message.

Clearly, shame is rooted in the lie that people can be and should be perfect. Where did we ever get such an idea? I don't think we were born with shame-carrying chromosomes. Therefore, I believe we learned shame in our earliest, most influential educational institution. We call it *the family*.

Please don't stop reading because you think I am going to tell you that all your current problems are your parents' fault. I am not saying that; I don't believe that. I believe that most of our parents simply parented in the way they were parented. In turn, we tend to parent the way our parents parented us. How else would they, or we, know how to parent?

But we must honestly examine our parents' parenting styles. Because, for better or for worse, *we live what we learn.*

It's true, isn't it? Just think about all the times we've discovered—

to our delight or dismay—that we were saying to our children the same things, with the same tone of voice, that we heard our parents say to us years before. We may have loved it or we may have hated it when we were kids. If the latter is true, we probably vowed we'd never say it when we got to be parents. But, day in and day out, we saw our parents' parenting style when we were children. And now, we may know no alternatives. We simply live what we learned.

Not only do we live what we learn, *we teach what we live.* Especially to our children. And our children will live what they learn about parenting from us. In other words, we are teaching our children to parent *their* children the way we are parenting *them.* And our children will teach our grandchildren how to be parents as our children live the parenting they learned from us.

Said differently, roots produce fruits "according to their kinds" (Gen 1:12). In turn, those fruits have seeds that sprout roots that produce more fruits "according to their kinds." Does that thought bring you pleasure or pain? If you're like me, it elicits some of both. And if you are racked with regret, believe me, I know that feeling too.

I've hauled bulging bags of shame and sorrow on many a gruesome guilt trip over my years of parenting. (I still do occasionally.) None of that did much to change me or my parenting. By itself, even genuine guilt fails to bring change. We must use that guilt to energize our examination of our parents' parenting of us so that we can see more clearly how to parent our children.

But this honesty enterprise raises a serious question for Christians who sincerely want to follow the biblical admonition to "honor" parents. How can we realistically re-view our parents' relationships with us as children and still not break God's commandment—especially if we suspect, or know, that our parents were not consistently adequate?

Honesty and "Honoring"
Surprisingly, because we are told to honor parents, we *must* acknowl-

edge their great influence on our lives and on our parenting. In Exodus 20:12, the original Hebrew word for "honor" referred to a very heavy object. When applied to people, it meant considering a person (such as a city official) influential or important, weighty.[1] We still describe influential people with the expression "he [or she] carries a lot of weight." And our parents' influence on us carries a lot of weight with us, both while we are growing up and in our adult lives.

So, if we say that our parents' behavior toward us has had little or no effect on us or on our behavior toward our children, we are in a sense dishonoring our parents. In reality—for good or ill—all parents are extremely influential in shaping the lives of all their children. Parents devoted to God, parents sold out to evil, and all the parents in between. We honor our parents most when we live in the light of this truth.

Of course, this truth means that, if we want to be more shame-free parents, we must admit that we are "heavy" in our own children's lives as we pass on many of the life-influencing parenting patterns that were passed on to us. Passing on intergenerational parenting patterns is just fine if our parents were *consistently adequate.* Please note that I did not say *perfect.* (There are no perfect people; since parents are people too, there are no perfect parents.)

In contrast, hand-me-down parenting patterns that are *shame-based* can be devastatingly destructive to us and to our children because of the seemingly endless cycle of harmful parenting roots producing parenting fruits that, in turn, sprout similar roots that produce more fruits. And on and on it goes.

Probably you are reading this book because you know or suspect that you grew up in a shame-based family. Perhaps, like me, you recognize that we really do live what we learn and we really do teach what we live. And, like me, you want to end that intergenerational cycle of shame. Clearly, our next step toward the goal of more shame-free parenting takes us back to our childhood families to see what we learned about life, about family and about parenting.

Roots of Shame-Bound Parenting

When we were babies, our immediate families were the entire universe. And as young children, we assumed that the way *our* families were was the way *all* families were—and were supposed to be.

Even many adults, especially those of us from shame-based families, are shocked when we discover that all parents do not scream at their children when they make mistakes, publicly ridicule them, compare them unfavorably with other children, expose them to pornography, emotionally abandon them, beat or rape them. Therefore, I am going to preface my discussion of shame-based families with a very brief overview of well-functioning families that are substantially (not totally) shame-free.

Recognizing Well-Functioning Families

Well-functioning, shame-free families are headed by substantially well-functioning, shame-free adults who are able to provide the security and stability their children need.

The children in these families learn that there is safety not only for their arms, legs and genitals, but for their ideas and aspirations. And because their parents are consistently responsible adults, children in these families are secure in the knowledge that they don't have to try to be adults. They are free to be children. In addition, even when serious problems arise, children in these families know that their parents will figure out what to do. That knowledge provides stability for the children when the family boat "rocks."

Actually, these parents *expect* personal and family problems because they have not bought into the lie that people should be perfect and problem-free. Therefore, when personal and family problems inevitably occur, they focus on problem solving.

Finally, and of crucial importance, these parents consistently tell the truth about what's going on in and around their families.

In contrast, shame-based families are headed by significantly shame-bound parents. The shame that binds these parents prevents them from acknowledging and resolving their own problems, and that impairs their capacity to provide consistently adequate parenting. However, parents' "disowned" problems are still present in their lives, and so they always profoundly influence the families these parents lead and the children they love.

These significantly impaired parents may be alcoholics, incest perpetrators and/or child or spouse batterers. But they also may be workaholics, rage-aholics, ridicule perpetrators and/or child or spouse neglecters. None of these problems is beyond solution. For example, alcoholics need to admit their problem, get help and stop ingesting alcohol. Incest perpetrators need to admit their problem, get help and stop molesting children. Do you see the pattern? Do you see the problem for shame-bound parents?

To *solve* problems, we have to let ourselves *see* problems. But shame says, "I should be perfect and problem-free." And since shame-bound parents believe that lie, they don't face personal and family problems and focus on problem solving. They focus on *appearance management.* There is an external focus in these families that teaches children that the way they, their parents and their families *look* is more important than the way they actually *are.* This is a kind of "image control" activity designed to conceal personal and family problems as opposed to solving them. So, for example, instead of admitting a problem and getting help, an alcoholic parent may justify the behavior as a response to job stress. A workaholic parent may do the same.

Finally, and tragically for their children, these parents consistently distort and deny what's happening in and around their families in order to preserve the illusion that "we are perfect, problem-free parents who have a perfect, problem-free family."

Figure 1-1 summarizes the basic differences between shame-free and shame-bound parents and families.

As we look more closely at shame-bound parents, we will see that they use five unspoken family rules to perpetuate the myth of personal and family perfection.

Family Functioning Comparison

Well-Functioning, Shame-Free Family	*Poorly Functioning, Shame-Bound Family*
1. Parents are substantially shame-free, so they don't expect to be perfect.	1. Parents are significantly shame-bound, so they believe they should be perfect.
2. Parents are consistently adequate because they admit personal problems and seek help to resolve them.	2. Parents are significantly impaired because they won't admit personal problems and seek help to resolve them.
3. Parents expect family problems, so when problems come, they focus on *problem solving.*	3. Parents expect family to be problem-free, so when problems come, they focus on *appearance management.*
4. Parents consistently tell the truth about what's happening in and around the family.	4. Parents consistently distort and deny what's happening in and around the family to conceal problems.

Figure 1-1.

Rules of Shame-Bound Parenting

As you read this brief description of the rules, you need to know that they all carry a "lifetime warranty." I mean that many people raised in shame-based families operate from this same set of rules throughout their entire lives.

Rule One: Be Blind. Specifically, children in shame-based families are expected to be blind to any perception of reality that contradicts the parents' "creative rearranging of facts." Real problems must be denied at all costs. And if we grew up in one of these families, we learned to be blind to the role reversals. We weren't supposed to see that we often functioned as "parentified" children in hopes of plugging the leadership gaps left by our "childified" parents.

Rule Two: Be Quiet. As children, we may have learned early that our families had a lot of secrets. It wasn't just that we didn't "air our dirty linen in public." We may have had secrets *within* the family too. (This is often true in incest families.) Obeying this rule means we reach neither outside the family to seek solutions to our problems nor inside the family to find support in our pain.

Rule Three: Be Numb. The unresolved problems in shame-bound families often create a chaotic atmosphere that stirs strong feelings in children. At the same time, parents in these families systematically teach their children to numb out emotions as, years before, these parents were taught to deaden their own feelings. Shame-bound parents also teach children to be numb to personal boundary violations. When parents beat, molest and/or discourage children from thinking for themselves, they violate their children's physical, sexual and intellectual boundaries.

Rule Four: Be Careful. When they are significantly impaired by unaddressed personal problems, even the most loving parents can become unpredictable and unreliable. And in that environment, children know their families are not truly safe. And clearly, children may wonder whether they can be safe *anywhere in the world* if they experience "hands-on" abuse like battering, confinement or sexual molestation in their very own homes. It doesn't take long for a child in a shame-bound family to learn that the only genuinely reliable person in the world is himself or herself.

Rule Five: Be Good. To understand this rule, you need to know that there are a lot of code words and phrases in shame-based families, and "good" is one of them. When applied to children in these families, the word *good* (as in "be good for Mommy") actually means "perfect"— or even "not a human child." And that makes a lot of sense when we consider the struggles of shame-bound parents.

The truth is that if parents are distracted by their own personal pain, the last thing they need or want is a real, human child with all his or her developmental limitations and legitimate needs. Impaired parents actually want and need children who can function as adults in meeting the parents' needs.

So, to earn the title of "good child" in a shame-based family, you had to (1) have no personal needs of your own, (2) have no critical (or even separate and different) thoughts and (3) know how to do everything correctly without being taught.

But perhaps most important, to qualify as "good" children—no matter what our ages—*we must remember nothing but the happy times!* As young children, we may have been like the five-year-old boy from an alcoholic home who, in the midst of a family crisis, said to his mother, "Don't worry, Mom, I won't remember this when I grow up." He knew what it took to be a "good child." But at five, he could not know that being a "good child" in a shame-bound family means not being a child at all. No wonder children from these families never feel "good enough."

Perhaps by now you recognize that your parents' parenting style was slightly or substantially shame-bound; you see the roots. Now the question is, how bountiful are the fruits?

Fruits of Shame-Bound Parenting

To begin evaluating your own parenting style, look over the statements in the following informal parenting quiz. Later we'll examine—"up close and personal"—many of the specific parenting challenges facing those of us from shame-bound families. This quiz may help us identify some of those challenges.

Parenting Evaluation Quiz

Scoring: 4 points for almost always (for example, I almost always think that/feel that . . .); 3 points for often; 2 points for occasionally; 1 point for almost never.

(1) _____ I feel undeserving of my children's love and trust.

(2) _____ I feel too overwhelmed and too underqualified to be a good parent.

(3) _____ I spend a lot of time justifying my children's behavior and accomplishments to my parents.

(4) _____ I use comparisons with other children to motivate my children to higher achievement.

(5) _____ I use ridicule, name-calling (e.g., "clumsy") and/or belittling with my children and then hate myself for doing it.

(6) _____ I leave my children with a parent or other family member even when I know that adult is emotionally and/or verbally abusive because I don't want to upset or anger that adult or "cause a problem" in the family.

(7) _____ I promise to spend "fun time" with my children but am too busy to follow through.

(8) _____ I've told my children that they really know how to make me mad and they finally believe me.

(9) _____ I think it's wrong to let my kids see me express strong feelings.

(10) _____ I spank my children and/or send them to their rooms when they cry for no good reason.

(11) _____ I call my college-age or adult children (or expect them to call me) almost every day.

(12) _____ I think telling children when they do things well makes them conceited.

(13) _____ I tell my children that God won't love them as much when they're disobedient.

(14) _____ I feel selfish when I do something just for myself.

(15) __2__ I think children who respect their elders will comply with their parents' wishes when it comes to choosing a church, a college, a career, etc.

(16) __1__ I leave my children alone with a parent or other family member even when I suspect that adult is physically and/or sexually abusive because I don't want to upset or anger that adult or "cause a problem" in the family. (Note: This is different from #6.)

(17) __1__ I think I would look weak if I ever apologized to my children or asked for forgiveness.

(18) __1__ I think it is impossible to know what children need.

(19) __1__ I let my parents or my spouse's parents have the final word about how we handle our children because they have more parenting experience than I/we do.

(20) __1__ I think it is more important to preserve my family's image/"witness" than to report my spouse/parent/grandparent/aunt/uncle for abusing my children or anyone else's children.

(21) __2__ I am uncomfortable touching/hugging my children because I don't know how to do it right.

(22) __4__ I've noticed that our family is too busy with church activities, or Little League, or piano lessons, etc. ad exhaustion, to sit down together for a family meal or a family meeting.

(23) __4__ I feel anxious when my children are around my parents/grandparents/aunts/uncles.

(24) __2__ I think it is far more important for children to listen to

their parents than for parents to listen to their children.

(25) _____ I read everything I can find about parenting but still feel like a total failure.

Scoring Key

25 points: You are too good to be true!

26-50 points: You are a consistently adequate parent. (But see note below.)

51-75 points: You are struggling with personal shame and shame-bound parenting.

Over 76 points: Your personal shame is significantly impairing your ability to be a consistently adequate parent. Please get help for yourself and your children.

Important note: If you answered anything other than "Almost Never" on statements 16 or 20, you and your children need help immediately.

How did you do with your "fruit inspecting"? Are you relieved and encouraged? Or do you feel overwhelmed with shock and sorrow from recognizing, perhaps for the first time, that you have reproduced the shame-bound parenting you received as a child?

Years ago, the ripe fruit of our parents' shame-bound parenting sowed seeds that germinated in the dark, fertile soil of human nature and neediness. The roots pushed through the cracks in our lives. We now see the fruit. And we dread the heavy harvest our children will reap "unto the third and fourth generations" and beyond.

Personal Reflection

Have you always believed that "honoring" your parents meant, "If you can't say anything nice don't say anything at all"? Are you willing to honestly evaluate your parents' "heavy" influence in your life? If not, what would it take for you to be willing?

Do you see the "fruits" of your parents' parenting style in your own parenting? If so, list some of them. If not, what are you doing differently?

Begin to list and evaluate the living and parenting rules you learned as a child. Which ones do you want to keep? Which do you want to modify or discard?

Looking Ahead

How do we end this shame-*full* cycle of sowing and reaping? Ignoring the fruit or hoping it will wither by itself doesn't seem to work. We need to cut it off at the roots. And to do that, we must recognize a fundamental parenting principle: only increasingly shame-free *people* can be increasingly shame-free *parents.*

Chapter two articulates the first implication of this principle.

2
Choosing
Life:
Recovering

A *perceptive bit of poetry captures some of the agony children (including some*
of us when we were children) can feel:
   god save the children
   trapped in the game
   living in fear
   hiding the pain
   battered by devils
   screaming in vain
   feeling the wrath
   then doing the same[1]
Recovering is about how to *stop* "doing the same" with our children.
   Therefore, recovering also must be about new choices. Not settling
in for the same old survival, bare-existence choices, but stretching out

for abundant, full-of-new-life choices. To do that, we must believe that we *should* and that we *could* choose life.

Indeed, God says we should. In the Old Testament, the Lord specifically gave the Israelites the option of following his ways to freedom and life or following "other gods" to bondage and death. And God gave an intergenerational incentive in Deuteronomy 30:19 when he called the people to *"choose life so that you and your children may live."*

Isn't that astounding? God is saying that when we, as *parents,* choose life, we open doors for our *children* to live and to choose life for themselves and their children.

A Parenting Parable

Actually, we hear this biblical principle proclaimed every time we get a flight attendant's safety speech. You know, all the instructions about emergency exits and flotation cushions that we usually ignore. Recently, I actually listened for a change, and I heard a parenting parable.

No, the flight attendant didn't say, "Choose life for yourselves and for your children." She said something like, "In case of a problem with the cabin pressure, oxygen masks will automatically be released. If you are traveling with small children, *secure your mask in place first and then secure your child's mask."*

Suddenly I saw it! The attendant's information about the oxygen masks was a parable with an unmistakable truth: *unless we first help ourselves by choosing life, we won't be able to help our children choose life.* But in shame-bound families, it is as if we, our parents and our children are all clutching our chests and choking on life-sapping lies and shame. Gagging and coughing, we gasp for deep, oxygen-rich breaths of truth and freedom. This choking sound becomes a deafening roar in some shame-bound families. In others, parents manage to stifle their gasps and carefully teach their children a more subdued, refined response to oxygen deprivation.

On our imaginary family-life flight, all these shame-bound parents and children wear various-sized earphones of denial that block information about the oxygen mask solution to air-pressure problems. In fact, these earphones play a tape saying, "You are flying in perfect, problem-free air pressure so you are expected to be perfect, problem-free breathers."

In this parenting parable, problems in air pressure are inevitable, so oxygen mask use is also inevitable. However, the shame-bound parents deny that choking or gasping is a problem. They explain to their children that this particular breathing pattern is a perfectly normal family characteristic.

In effect, these parents are saying to their children, "Air pressure problems? Not here. We don't know what you're talking about—you must be crazy. You say your lungs burn from oxygen deprivation? There you go again, always thinking about yourself and making such a big deal out of everything. And stop worrying about turning blue, that's just what happens in our family. Hey, look at us; we're blue too and we're not griping about it. We look good in blue."

As children in shame-bound families, most of us never learned that we could reach for life-giving change. Few, if any, adults in the family even told us about the oxygen masks, let alone modeled one for us.

Since you are reading this book, you have at least begun to remove the earphones of denial and hear about the fresh air of freeing truth. But the idea of focusing on your own oxygen needs may seem incredibly selfish when you're so concerned about your children's oxygen supply. (You may remember actually questioning the wisdom of the flight attendant's instructions the first time you heard them on a real plane. I know I did.)

It's as if, clutching our throats and nearly unconscious, we gasp, "I can't be bothered spending time and effort on *my* breathing. Just tell me how to help my *children* breathe better." This is when we must hear the parable's message: "If you do not reach for the oxygen when you need it, you will not be *able* to help your children, no matter how much you love them."

A recent University of Utah study found, not surprisingly, that depressed mothers were less attentive and emotionally engaged with their children than non-depressed mothers.[2] And I remember only too well how emotionally unavailable I was to my young children years ago when I was deeply depressed for many months. In fact, I was so depressed that my family physician referred me to a psychiatrist.

My first response to that doctor's suggestion sounded exactly like our imaginary parent. I didn't think my emotional condition was important enough to warrant paying a psychiatrist's fee. I sincerely believed that, in spite of the fact that I was sleeping between fourteen and eighteen hours every day. I also was in enormous physical pain, and my physician said I was irreparably damaging my body. In addition, my husband encouraged me to go and we had excellent medical insurance.

Do you know what finally made me choose to see a psychiatrist, take medication and endure the painful therapy process? I did it for my son and daughter. Depression had destroyed my capacity to care about myself, but it had not depleted my love for my young children. I did not want to continue sleeping away their childhoods. In effect, *my choice to become a healthier parent forced me to become a healthier person!*

What if our children are older—old enough to reach, as it were, for their own oxygen masks? Even adult children usually look to their parents to see what's permissible and possible. Many of us do that with our parents, even if we don't readily acknowledge it.

We also may not recognize or acknowledge that our older children look to us to see what they should and could do and be. This is all the more reason to breathe deeply of truth. In the parable's language, our oxygen-poor grown children won't be convinced of oxygen's life-giving benefits unless they see the changes it brings in our breathing.

In our parable, the act of reaching for the oxygen mask represents

Ask about after School care
possibility — How much more
money.

choosing life. As parents, we can continue the shame-bound family tradition of "turning blue" and raising children who "turn blue." Or we can choose something healthier than our parents chose. But remember, God and the flight attendant both want us to know that *parents' choices affect their children.*

This is true, in part, because children don't have the same range of choices adults have. We must feel the potentially devastating impact of this reality to grasp our need for recovering.

Childhood Choices and "Stumbling"

I grew-up in an English-speaking family, so that means that I learned to think and speak in English. It also means that I couldn't wake up one morning and suddenly decide to think and speak in French. In effect, I lived in an English-speaking universe because I didn't even know that French, or any other languages, existed. Having no alternative source of information about language as a child, I had no choice but to think and speak in my parents' language.

Now suppose that my parents not only taught me to think and speak in English but also taught me that English was the only real, correct, good, valuable, moral, worthwhile language in which to think and speak. Having no alternative source of information about language as a child, I would have no choice but to believe that their statements reflected reality.

Suppose further that when I got a little older I noticed that some families did not always think and speak in English and I asked my parents to explain. What do you think would have happened if they had told me, subtly or brutally, that I was stupid and/or crazy for even thinking about the possibility of using another language? And what if my parents also implied that I was disloyal to even raise the issue and that if I wanted to stay a part of *their* family I had better learn to think and speak the way *they* did. Having no alternative source of family (food, shelter, relationship), I would have no choice but to buy my parents' presentation of reality. The alternative—

abandonment—would be life-threatening for a child.

So, self-protectively and unknowingly, I would choose to adopt my parents' English-only perceptual grid. From then on, every experience in or out of the family would be filtered through that interpretive grid. Even as an adult, to be a "loyal" child and avoid the pain of my parents' emotional abandonment, I would automatically filter out other language choices.

When parents and other adults give children a false perception of reality, that becomes an obstacle that makes children "stumble." Because they believe these lies are truth and act on them, the children can experience disastrous personal and spiritual consequences.

Again we see the powerful way in which parents' choices affect their children. This truth applies to our parents' choices affecting us and to our choices affecting our children.

Understanding the Recovering Process
What happens when we are caused to "stumble" by learning a language of lies that shapes our childhood perceptions and choices? To one degree or another, we get hurt.

If we were caused to stumble over a thirty-foot cliff, we may discover that we are covered with blood where broken bones protrude through our torn flesh. Or if we stumbled off a three-inch curb, perhaps only one knee is skinned. In both cases, or anything in between, we are not responsible, as children, for being caused to stumble into the misperceptions of reality that shaped our subsequent self-protective choices. However, that may be small comfort when we begin to evaluate the injuries we've sustained—and *inflicted*—as a result of our stumbling and choosing.

Besides, the critical question now is: how do we learn to walk again, or at least to use a wheelchair? The concept of rehabilitative medicine provides the answer, I believe. With physical therapy, nearly all accident survivors learn to walk again or master wheelchair use. But recovery is never something that just *happens to* these accident survivors. It requires hard work, and patients always have to *actively participate* in this recovery process.

There are obvious implications for those of us who were caused to stumble as children. Significant recovery will not take place without our painful and determined participation. That may seem extraordinarily unfair since we were not to blame for the original wounding lies, whether great or small. But recovering is not about placing blame. It is about making new, healthier, more truth-based and life-giving choices now than we could make as children.

Clearly, we must attribute appropriate responsibility to our parents' powerful influences in our childhood choices. *But now as adults, we—not our parents—are responsible for our choices.*

Our parents will always *influence* us, but they cannot *control* us without our cooperation. We have a far wider range of choices now, as adults. So if our parents are still controlling us today, it is only because we are choosing to allow it. We may not know we are choosing that, but we are.

Somewhere along the path to adulthood, we chose to continue relating to our parents and to the world as if we were still children without choices. In effect, we unknowingly chose to "grow down" instead of grow up. Therefore, when we now choose recovery, we are reclaiming the power of personal choice that, years ago, we sacrificed on the altar of self-protection and parental approval.

When we choose to stop "doing the same" with our children, we necessarily choose the hard work of recovering from our own family lies and childhood shame-wounds. And we have seen that we *should* do that, because God urges us to choose life for ourselves and our children. So, we've answered the "should-we-choose-life" question with which we began.

But the "could-we" question remains. Twenty-five years ago, my intense, prayerful desire to stop "doing the same" with my children overcame paralyzing clinical depression and launched me into a lifelong recovering process of making and practicing new choices. Many times this choosing and changing process seemed too difficult and painful. At those times, I would have given up on choosing a healthier life for myself if I had not cared so deeply about choosing a healthier life for my children.

In the following chapters, you will hear about many other parents who have answered the "could-we-choose-life" question with a thunderous, "Yes, we can—and God will guide us!" Ask God to help you believe that. And ask him to take your love for your children, whatever their ages, and use it to strengthen your commitment to your own recovering process. Remember, only increasingly shame-free people can be increasingly shame-free parents.

Personal Reflection

As you ponder the parenting parable, ask yourself these questions:
☐ Are you wearing "earphones of denial"?
☐ If so, how large are they and what messages are they playing?
☐ Are you or your children "turning blue" from shame? (If you aren't sure, review the traits and rules of shame-bound parents and families in chapter one.)
☐ If so, what do you need to do to help yourself and your children?

Looking Ahead

You are reading this book because you care about becoming a more shame-free parent. If that requires your commitment to becoming a more shame-free person, and if shame is based on a lie, then you must also commit to choosing truth. Let's talk about that next.

3
Choosing Truth: Re-viewing

*E*very *significant break*through *requires a significant break*-with. *So, to* achieve a breakthrough in our lives and our parenting, we often must break with old family messages so we can choose truth.

Choosing truth means we must be willing to *break with* our parents' living and parenting practices when these practices are rooted in lies and shame. However, choosing truth does *not* mean we automatically assume that our parents are monsters and that everything they ever taught us is a lie. That approach reflects the all-or-nothing, thinking-in-extremes pattern that pervades most shame-bound families.

In contrast, Scripture tells us to examine everything carefully and hold onto only that which is intrinsically good, right and true. (See 1 Thess 5:21.) This is a call to replace our "shame grid" with a "truth grid." To do that, we will need to review our past and present experiences, our perceptions of them and the choices we made in response. I mean, literally, *re*-view: look again. However, to many people that prospect seems vaguely dangerous or even sinful.

The Need for Re-viewing

Throughout Scripture, God calls his people to unsparing inner honesty. This isn't surprising when we consider that God reveals himself as a God of truth. Jesus referred to himself as Truth and declared that real freedom is a by-product of knowing and choosing truth. (See, for example, Eph 4:25 and Jn 8:32.)

Facing and following truth is an unfamiliar process for those of us raised in shame-based families where facade took precedence over facts. However, avoiding reality by distortion and denial will never change the facts of our childhoods or the impact of those facts on our lives and our parenting.

If we were raised in extremely dysfunctional families, truth was not just a stranger; *truth was an enemy.* But when we long to be more shame-free parents, we must embrace this childhood enemy. When we don't, we imperil both ourselves and our children.

I recently met a lovely Christian woman I will call Karen. (Names and details have been changed in all the real-life experiences I describe in this book.) Through sobs Karen told me that two of her three children remember being severely abused by her parents. The children didn't feel safe enough to tell Karen about the abuse until after her father's death, because Karen's father and mother had threatened to kill Karen if her children told.

"I would never have left them alone so much with my folks if I had known about my own childhood abuse," Karen wailed. "The kids didn't tell me about *their* abuse until after I began to remember *mine.*"

When, as an adult, Karen repressed (unknowingly denied) the ghastly truth of her physical and sexual abuse, she was still living with her childhood perception (accurate at the time) of personal

powerlessness and limited choice. She couldn't see that those perceptions and choices were now obsolete and that they were actually
harmful. In unknowingly ignoring her own personal pain she was
putting her children at risk.

Certainly, most parents do not have such devastatingly clear evidence of the need to re-view childhood experiences, perceptions and
choices. And most parents do not have such devastatingly painful
childhood experiences to hide from their adult awareness. Yet, according to the Bible, we all have *some* unrecognized and disowned
inner parts that are hidden from us. And God wants us to have truth
there too.

How can we be expected to have truth in an unseen part of ourselves? I believe God provides the answer in Psalm 51:6. In that verse,
the Lord reveals his desire for us to have truth in our innermost being,
and he promises to give us wisdom in the "hidden part" (KJV) of our
inner selves.

So, when my question is, "How can I possibly re-view and choose
truth about something significant to my shame-free parenting goal
if it is hidden in some inner territory I don't even know I own?"
God's answer seems to be, "I will give you the wisdom you need, to
know what you will need to know, so that you can choose the truth
I want you to have in your life."

If we have ever tried in vain to change other people's choices, we
know that *we can't change what we can't choose.* Furthermore, we *don't know*
we can change what we *don't know* we have chosen. Therefore, recognizing and reclaiming ("owning") our choices is a prerequisite to changing our living and parenting choices. Figure 3-1 depicts the changes in
choice ownership that occur as we allow God to give us wisdom in
the "hidden part" of ourselves. This change process is a key component
in our progress toward shame-free living and parenting.

As children, our most basic choice is: stay alive. All subsequent
choices reflect this foundational one, in the sense that they are life-
affirming and self-protective.

Recovering Choice Ownership

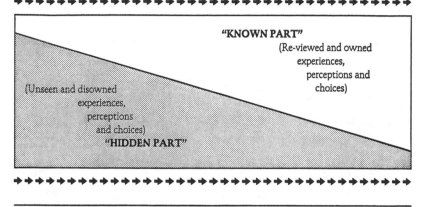

Figure 3-1.

Each of us grew up in a unique family universe. This reality reflects the wide range of family functioning, from virtually idyllic "Cosby Show" homes all the way to those resembling Nazi death camps. Whatever the quality of their families' health, young children tend to be excellent observers of these family worlds. However, because of limited cognitive development, children are not so skilled at interpreting their worlds.

I have noticed some striking similarities in the perceptions and interpretations we tend to form when growing up on the dysfunctional end of the family functioning continuum. Perhaps this is because infants in these families sense that their safety and security are in question, to one degree or another. If so, we may assume that these infants, to one degree or another, also begin to focus on staying alive by keeping themselves safe, rather than being able to explore and enjoy a safe and secure universe created by consistently adequate parents.

Unfortunately, these inaccurate early perceptions shape the life-affirming, self-protective choices we make. In turn, these choices shape much of who we become as people and as parents. And this is precisely why we must *re*-view our distorted childhood perceptions and choices if we are going to choose truth.

Re-viewing Childhood

Figure 3-2 summarizes substantially shame-*free* childhood experiences, perceptions, choices and consequent adult parenting choices. Compare it with figure 3-3, an overview of three levels of shame-*bound* childhood experiences and the probable perceptions and choices they triggered. As children we tended to receive our parents' treatment of us as messages about our identity and worth. So I have included the "parental message" a child would probably receive from each level of treatment.

As you examine these two charts, ask God to give you wisdom in the "hidden part" of your inner being. Then listen inside for a whispered or shouted "this-sounds-familiar" response.

Shame-Free Childhood Experiences, Perceptions and Choices
Basic Choice of All Children: Stay Alive

Childhood Experience	Parental Message	Childhood Perception	Childhood Choices	Adult/Parent Choices
Child sees the parents' developmental superiority. Parents understand child development and encourage the child to grow, learn to think for him/herself and become a separate person. Parents consistently provide adequate parenting.	You're a precious human child. You are just great the way you are and it is great when you grow and change. We will meet your needs and care for you until you can do that for yourself. We will always love you no matter how much you grow and change.	My parents know everything about everything and always tell the truth. They think I am great when I do/learn new things. They will always love me and will take care of me until I can take care of myself.	I will grow and learn and try new thoughts and behaviors. Because I love my parents, I will try to please them, but even when I do not please them, my parents will still love me.	I will use some of my parents' "rules" when they are helpful. Since neither my parents nor the rules are perfect, I will choose different rules too. My parents won't mind. *Therefore, I will parent as my parents did in some ways and differently in other ways.*

Figure 3-2.

Levels of Shame-Based Childhood Experiences, Perceptions and Choices

Basic Choice of All Children: Stay Alive

	Childhood Experience	Parental Message	Childhood Perception	Childhood Choices	Adult/Parent Choices
Some Shame	Child sees the parents' developmental superiority. Parents use disrespect and dogmatism to reinforce their lifelong superiority.	You're *just* a human child. Children are *never* as strong and as smart as their parents.	My parents know everything about everything and always tell the truth. They will *always* know more than I do, so I will *always* need them to be safe.	I will figure out how to please my parents so they will continue to protect and direct me. I will *always* be safer living by all my parents' rules.	Parents' rules rule forever. I am bad or stupid when I want to do anything differently. Something bad would happen if I ever did. *Therefore, I will parent as my parents did.*
Much Shame	Child sees significant family chaos of repeated crises from consistently inadequate parental leadership. Parents don't get help for their problems because of shame lie. Child's legitimate needs are consistently neglected.	You have to be *more* than a human child. We "can't take" the pressure of trying to meet your needs and ours too. Our needs are more important than yours, because we are the parents. So, don't expect your needs to be met.	My parents "can't take" the truth about my real feelings or needs or anything else. When my parents feel better, I feel safer. I make my parents feel better when I have *no* real child needs. I am "selfish" and "cause trouble" when I do have personal needs.	I will have to protect, shield and "fix" my parents. I have to take care of them so they can take care of me and keep me safe.	I will protect and please my parents and other important people in my life so they will like/love me and I'll feel safe. I would hurt my parents and "cause trouble" by doing things differently. *Therefore, I will parent as my parents did.*
Enormous Shame	Child receives "hands-off" abuse (e.g., ridicule, unfavorable comparisons, name-calling) and "hands-on" abuse (e.g., beating, incest, confinement). Parents don't get help for their problems because of shame lie.	You are *less* than a human child. You are such a disgustingly different and disappointing child, you deserve to receive the treatment we are giving you.	My parents know what/who I am and are good/right to treat me as they do. I need my parents to be good/right because they are the only ones I have to take care of me. I feel safer when I have "good" parents who treat their children the way they deserve.	I will believe that I am bad and worth *less* than other children so that I can have "good" parents to care for me and keep me safe. I will try to be good enough to earn less painful treatment.	I must take or do anything to earn the right to have people/parents in my life so that I can feel safe from abandonment. I am bad, stupid and evil. My parents are good and right. *Therefore, I will parent as my parents did.*

Figure 3-3.

As you can see, shame-bound childhood experiences tend to bind adult children into rigid patterns of parenting as they were parented. Sometimes these adult children raise their own families very differently than they themselves were raised. But without some personal recovering work, this often is more of a knee-jerk reaction than a well-considered response to new parenting information. That was Arnold's experience.

"I was determined to raise my children in the exact opposite way from how I was raised." Arnold said vehemently. "And boy oh boy, did I ever! My folks were unbelievably strict about absolutely everything, so I decided to be pretty loose about most things. When we visited my folks and they criticized my leniency with the kids, that just made me even more lenient. Now I realize I was trying to hurt my folks by showing them that I thought they were wrong— but I ended up hurting my kids by not disciplining them." Then he added wistfully, "Now these kids are adults, and they tell me they always thought I didn't *care* enough about them to set limits! And I see how destructive their lack of self-discipline is—and it nearly kills me."

Clearly, we don't achieve shame-free parenting either by mindlessly repeating our parents' ways or by reflexively doing the exact opposite. The best choice is consistent with the biblical admonition to examine everything carefully and retain what is good and true.

Re-viewing Parenting Lies and Truths

Let's summarize the parenting principles and expectations underlying the three levels of shame-bound childhood experiences. We will then compare them with more realistic and truthful principles and expectations used in essentially shame-free families.

Remember, shame-bound living and parenting are rooted in the lie that says adults ought to be perfect and problem-free and there is something different and uniquely wrong with us if we are not. This lie even has a special parenting corollary that says: children ought to

Shame-Bound Parenting Lies

Shame-Free Parenting Truths

1. My parents are "giant geniuses" who will *always* be smarter and stronger than I am.

1. Parents are older human beings. This means they have more information and physical strength than children. Under normal circumstances, children will be about as smart (or smarter) and as strong (or stronger) someday.

2. I was selfish and caused trouble as a child when I had personal needs of my own that inconvenienced my parents.

2. All children have legitimate personal needs that often inconvenience their parents. This is one of the realities of parenting.

3. My parents are supposed to protect and direct me *forever* since they will *always* know more than I know.

3. My parents were supposed to protect and direct me when I was young. As I got older, my parents were supposed to teach me how to protect myself in most situations and how to seek God's protection and direction in all situations.

4. My parents are supposed to love me more when I obey them and make them look good.

4. I should not have to earn my parents' love. Parents are supposed to love their children unconditionally.

5. I am supposed to make my parents happy.

5. I do not have the power to make my parents or anybody else happy any more than anybody else has the power to make me happy.

6. I am supposed to please my parents, and if I work hard enough and/or am good enough, I will be able to please my parents.

6. "Being pleased" is a function of my parents' personal value system. I am supposed to live to please God. This may or may not please my parents too.

7. I am supposed to meet all my parents' needs and give them a reason to feel good about themselves, i.e., "fix" them.

7. I do not have the power to "fix" my parents or any other person. (God doesn't need children to "fix" parents. He already sent Jesus to do that!)

8. My parents accurately assessed my intrinsic worth and their treatment of me is a commentary about my true identity.

8. I, and all human beings, have intrinsic worth because we are made in the image of God. Therefore, all human beings deserve respectful treatment. My parents' treatment of me is a commentary about *them,* not about *me.*

9. Loyal, loving and respectful children will always follow their parents' parenting rules since their parents were perfect (or almost perfect).

9. Being a loyal, loving, respectful child does not mean I must pretend that either my parents or their rules are perfect. Lying is not loving.

Figure 3-4.

be able to act like adults. Look for the shame-roots in the lies listed in figure 3-4. And let yourself begin to experience the freedom inherent in the contrasting truths.

After comparing parenting lies and parenting truths, we are confronted with the "rival-rulers crisis." In Matthew 6:24, Jesus declared the impossibility of serving two rulers, or "masters," because we will end up hating one and loving the other. This is true whether the opposing "rulers" are money and God or lies and truth.

Lies or Truth?

The critical question in all "rival-rulers crises" is: *whose rules rule?* In the "rival-rulers crisis" between parenting lies and parenting truths, our answer determines the difference between passing on the intergenerational "baton of shame" or ending that wretched relay with truth. Here are two examples of how that works.

Connie, a Christian woman from an "enormous shame" family, often babysits for her two nieces. Recently, she was horrified to discover welts and bruises on them, and she immediately confronted their mother, her unmarried older sister. Here's Connie's description of their conversation and the aftermath.

"I asked my sister what happened to the girls. She just shrugged and said that her new boyfriend lost his temper with them. When I told my sister she ought to protect her kids, she told me it was 'no big deal.' My sister said that we had all survived our dad's beating us and her kids would survive too. At first I thought maybe she was right and I was making too big a deal of it. But then I decided her girls were too sweet to deserve that, so I called child protective services. My sister was furious at me—still won't speak to me. She told my folks and now they're furious too. I don't care. I just know those girls deserve better than being beaten."

Connie faced the "rival-rulers crisis" and truth won. She had participated in a Christian recovery group for adult children from dysfunctional families, and she credits that group for helping her realize that adults' treatment of children is not automatically justified.

Unfortunately, groups like that didn't exist when *my* children were young.

I have concluded that my childhood experiences fluctuated between the "some shame" and the "much shame" levels most of the time, although there were a few isolated "enormous shame" experiences of life-threatening violence and sexual molestation.

Whatever the level of family chaos, I lived day in and day out operating from this principle: "I am supposed to make my mother happy and make her feel good (or at least *better)* about herself and her life." Unfortunately for me and for my children, no one told me that was impossible because it was rooted in a lie. So I became the classic "hero" in an alcoholic family: straight A's, piano recital at five, and so on. And I also became the classic shame-bound and shame-passing parent that lethally loyal "heroes" usually grow up to be.

One of my most painful parenting memories is a vivid testimonial to the die-hard staying power of the parenting lie I lived as a child. It occurred during a week I spent with my mother and her new husband in Arizona when our son, Dave, was about three and a half and our daughter, Becky, was a year old. We were living in Seattle during those years, so the visit entailed all the stress of flying with small children and setting up the child-care routine in a strange home.

Dave was thrilled to ride his grandparents' pony. However, he was not so thrilled with all of his new surroundings and schedule—and he made that crystal-clear. I grew increasingly anxious when he exhibited, with annoying regularity, that he was not a perfect child. I thought I was being appropriately firm, even though I did tolerate more fussiness than when we were at home. But, clearly, that did not make the correct statement about my mother. (Note: not about Dave or about me. About *my mother.*)

Two days into the visit, she delivered a subtle reminder which reactivated my childhood guiding principle. Mother took me aside and said, "I read somewhere that you never *really* know what kind of parent you are until you have grandchildren. When I see you and Dave, well—it makes me wonder."

Of course! How could I have missed it? I wasn't making my mother feel good about herself and her mothering when I allowed my child to behave like the overstimulated, confused three-year-old he was. I did not have any "inner-parts" wisdom back then, so I lacked the decoding key I needed to fully decipher my mother's hero-activating message. But, sad to say, I got the original meaning loud and clear. And as soon as I got it, my poor son "got it" too!

It never occurred to me to do anything other than immediately clamp down on my three-year-old as if he had just appeared on the FBI's "Most Wanted" list. Oh, he became more subdued and docile, all right. (Now I realize that was probably due to a combination of shock and terror.) I scrutinized Dave's every waking moment for telltale signs of imperfection. And I did such a thorough job that by the end of the week I had earned my mother's "seal of approval" for noteworthy child improvement.

Was my mother a monster? Absolutely not. My mother deeply loved me and my children. Yet my mother was also a very deeply shame-wounded woman who looked to her children, and later her grandchildren, to mend her tattered self-concept. Mother's parents had unintentionally inflicted her earliest shame-wounds. And those wounds were seen most clearly in my mother's incapacity to sustain a healthy, mutually respectful and responsible marriage.

First, Mother unknowingly married a bigamist and embezzler who was in a federal prison by the time I, their daughter, was born. There she was in 1938: three thousand miles from her family, with few friends, and now a single parent—long before it became fashionable.

At the hospital where I was born and where she worked, rumors flew about my illegitimacy. I understood more clearly the depth of my mother's humiliation and sense of shame when, last year shortly before her death, she told me about tacking her wedding license to the main hospital bulletin board to quell those rumors. I am still moved to tears when I think of the personal pain that motivated her action.

And as if her first marriage were not sufficiently esteem-puncturing, two years later she married the alcoholic stepfather I believed was my biological father until I was ten. That marriage survived eleven years and produced one son.

After I married and left home, Mother married three more times (but just two husbands). The situation I described with Dave came during her first marriage to husband number three.

You see, none of us were monsters. My mother's parents, my mother and I—*all* loved our children. That's the point—and the tragedy. We were all just shame-bound, loyal and loving adult children of shame-bound parents who dutifully passed along the intergenerational baton of shame when it came to our lap of that wretched relay.

Loving our children is not enough! Those of us from shame-based families need a new perspective and a shift of loyalties if we are to end the shame-passing and become substantially shame-free parents.

My Child's Parent or My Parent's Child?
I had to learn to be more concerned about meeting my young children's needs than my mother's needs. I realize all of this now, but didn't when that "loyalty encounter" occurred. I deeply regret not recognizing it till eight years later.

When I finally did shift into a parent-of-my-child mindset instead of primarily a child-of-my-parent perspective, I had to change a lot of my rules. And so will you if your parents' rules have ruled automatically. This can be extremely difficult but it is absolutely essential, because the rules we follow become a life map.

An ancient Chinese proverb states: *If we do not change our direction, we are apt to end up where we are headed.* How true. And how tragic, if we are mapping our lives with lies and shame. This is doubly tragic for us as parents, since we are not traveling alone. But this is doubly hopeful too. When we adopt more accurate life maps by choosing truth, to one degree or another depending on their ages, we will piggyback our children on this journey to more shame-free living.

Personal Reflection

Study the charts in figures 3-2 and 3-3.
□ Can you locate your birth family's shame level?
□ How about the family you have created for your children?
  Look over the list of lies and truths in figure 3-4. Which column contains more of your life-guiding principles?
□ Do you need to resolve a "rival-rulers crisis"?
□ What do you need to do to come down on the side of truth?
□ Are you willing to do it? If not, why not?

Looking Ahead

Often there are some unpleasant and unwelcome side effects to choosing truth and receiving hidden-part wisdom about the parenting we have inherited and perpetuated. Specifically, we may begin to experience deep resentment toward our parents and even ourselves.

If this is true for you, remember that choosing truth is not complete without also choosing grace.

4
Choosing
Grace:
Releasing

*I*n *her delightful book* Growing Up with My Children, *Ellen Walker*
credits William Hazlitt with saying:

> Man is the only animal that laughs and weeps; for he is the only
> animal that is struck with the difference between what things are
> and what they might have been.[1]

If we are committed to choose truth by re-viewing our pasts, some
of us may feel a lot more like weeping than laughing when we
ponder "the difference between what things are and what they
might have been."

We have seen that choosing truth requires choosing grace. The
biblical meaning of grace is that of giving a gift and indicates things
which bring well-being.[2] As long as truth confronts us with the
striking difference between what is and what might have been, and

as long as we have no one but imperfect human beings populating our families, we will need to operate in the relational realm by grace. We do that by receiving and giving the gift of *release.*

It is impossible to fully reach for hopeful tomorrows with both hands full of yesterday's resentments and regrets. Therefore in our journey to shame-free living and parenting, we need to release those resentments and regrets about "what might have been" so we can embrace the reality of what is and pursue the potential of what can be.

In both sacred and secular literature, there is another word often used for release: *forgive.* These terms are closely related in the New Testament; in fact, "let go" and "release" are the primary definitions of the two most common Greek words translated "forgive."[3] Unfortunately, many people—especially many Christians—have distorted ideas about forgiveness.

Sadly, some of us promote denial and participate in revictimization in the name of "forgiveness," when those actions clearly contradict both truth and grace. For this reason, we need to carefully examine the releasing function of forgiveness.

What Forgiving Is
I use a simple, three-step description of the forgiving process: face it, feel it, forgive it. The starting point is truth.

1. Forgiving is recognizing our injury. When we begin to consider forgiving, we are saying that someone *really* hurt us—it is not just in our imaginations. It is admitting to ourselves, "Yes, someone *did* shove me off a four-inch curb." Or, "That's right, I remember being hurled off a forty-foot cliff. I was terrified then and I hurt now." Whether or not the offending party *intended* to injure us is not the issue. The point is, they did.

2. Forgiving is reclaiming our responses. When children are hurt by their parents or other significant caretakers, the children usually respond with feelings of anger, fear and sadness. But in shame-bound families, children learn to bury those legitimate human emotions because parents usually make it clear that feelings in general, and the "threatening three" (anger, fear and sadness) in particular, are unacceptable.

Those emotions are unacceptable to our shame-bound parents because they suggest that the family might not really be perfect and problem-free. Besides, our shame-bound parents probably learned years before in *their* shame-bound families that those feelings were "bad." So, in effect, we learn to disown or deaden our emotional responses to hurtful, shame-based childhood experiences.

We may learn to deaden them with mood-altering substances or activities. I believe this is the primary purpose of all "addictions": to anesthetize unacceptable emotions.

For example, I have counseled with many incest survivors who used food to self-medicate the painful feelings they weren't ready to own. Now, I don't want to oversimplify here. Undereating or overeating can serve other purposes, such as making the incest survivor's body less attractive, by cultural standards, and thereby making her feel safer. The point is that these women did not begin to eat in more healthy ways until *after* recovering the repressed memories of their childhood abuse and reclaiming their emotional responses.

And there was one more component, an absolutely essential one, to the forgiving process that brought these people personal peace and emotional healing.

3. *Forgiving is giving up the right to retaliate.* This is where grace enters the scene—center stage. Rage, resentment and bitterness fuel the desire for revenge, but they also consume enormous amounts of emotional energy. Releasing the right to "get revenge" frees us to redirect all that energy into healing instead of hating and hurting. But it's not just efficient energy use; it's *necessary.* Releasing is a must, not only because we are choosing grace, but because we've chosen to live in truth.

Ask yourself, "What could I possibly do now to get even for what happened to me this morning, last week or twenty years ago?" I mean, just *exactly* even. How could we know if we've hurt the person or persons enough to *precisely* equal our hurt? Certainly, we don't want to be guilty of hurting them *more* than they hurt us. See what I mean?

Am I saying that they ought to be allowed to "get away with it"? I am not saying that at all. No one ever "gets away with" sin! And certainly we don't forgive in order to free others of responsibility for their sins against us. We could not do that even if we wanted to—God and reality will not allow it.

Instead, we forgive to free ourselves of resentment for their sins against us. And when we forgive, we are not dumping those sinful deeds and their doers into a dark pit of denial. We are redirecting the desire for private reprisal by releasing those sins and those sinners into the nail-scarred hands of the ultimate Judge—God.

What Forgiving Is Not

I hope it is clear that I do not think forgiving is synonymous with denying. We need to understand what else forgiving is *not*, lest we take ourselves and our children down a deceptive and dangerous path.

1. Forgiving is not discounting the pain. I've already said that forgiving is not denying that something hurtful happened. Even more, forgiving is not talking and acting as if nothing serious happened. When we do that, we discount ourselves and our pain. It is true that our childhood perceptions of many events are unrealistic because children have limited understanding of the world. However, children know when they have physical or emotional pain. And children and their pain deserve to be respected, not discounted. This is true of us and our own past childhoods, as well as of other children.

2. Forgiving is not excusing because we "understand." Have you ever noticed that many people who are confronted with their wrongdoing say something like "You just don't understand"? They often explain and explain in an effort to make us "understand," as if understanding a behavior makes that behavior acceptable. It doesn't!

We may understand the painful dynamics that motivate previously molested men and women to become child molesters, but we do not excuse or condone their behavior just because we understand it. When someone says, "If you really understood, you'd forgive me," that person betrays a misunderstanding of forgiveness. We must confront the challenge of forgiving precisely because excusing, condoning and "understanding" do not effectively release us from past hurts.

3. Forgiving is not forgetting facts or feelings. Amnesia is not an automatic aftermath of forgiveness. Unfortunately, there is a myth that says if we forgive, we must forget. Deep emotional injuries rarely disappear from our memories once we recall them. And the strong emotions that accompany hurtful memories often "blow us off course" even when we have sincerely "set our sail" for forgiving. This doesn't mean we are not honest forgivers; it means we are human forgivers.

Let's face it, we humans are a lot more at home with grudges than with grace. Forgiving goes against our natural desire for justice—the "eye for an eye, tooth for a tooth" kind of scale-balancing justice. In fact, many of us have wandered around, blind and toothless, for a long time before we got desperate enough to ask God to give us the grace to forgive.

4. Forgiving is not something we do by ourselves. I am convinced that genuine, life-changing releasing/forgiving is not something we would ever think up or be able to accomplish without the supernatural power of God working in us.

To be honest, I would never even have *thought* about forgiving my biological father's betrayal of me (he wanted to abort me) and of my mother if my heavenly Father had not proposed the idea. And I assure you that I would never have done it if God had not empowered my faltering desire to obey his call to forgive as I had been forgiven. (See, for example, Mk 11:25; Eph 4:32; Col 3:13.)

5. Forgiving is not the same as reconciliation. When I forgave my father, I had no idea if he was living or dead, let alone how to contact him. I had no way to tell him I'd forgiven him or to seek reconciliation.

Does that mean I did not truly forgive? Some people seem to think that we haven't forgiven unless we have reconciled with the person who hurt us. I see it differently.

Here are some helpful words to untangle this knotty issue.

Forgiveness is an *inner* response; reconciliation is a *behavioral* coming together. I can forgive an abusive spouse by not seeking retaliation; I would not reconcile until I am sure that the destructive behavior will not happen again. Forgiveness includes a *willingness* to reconcile, waiting in hope that the other changes. Reconciliation, of course, may be a result of forgiveness, but is not an inevitable step.[4]

I agree. And I believe this is a scriptural approach to forgiveness, because the biblical basis for reconciliation is mutual acceptance of truth. God loves us and, in his grace, has provided forgiveness for our sins through Jesus. But unless we respond to God's grace and agree with him that we have sinned and *need* forgiveness, there is no mutual acceptance of truth and no basis for reconciliation.

Because forgiveness is an inward releasing of our hurts and our hurters, no one can stop us from forgiving. However, hurters can short-circuit reconciliation by denying the truth about their actions.

When these unrepentant, denying hurters are in our families, they usually expect us to resume playing the "let's-pretend-nothing-happened" game even after we have remembered and re-viewed their hurtful behavior. If we believe that genuine forgiveness demands instantaneous, boundary-less reconciliation, we will be sitting ducks for further victimization. And so will our children. Furthermore, when we knowingly deny the truth and allow actively abusing people to continue sinning against us and others, we disobey God's command to "have nothing to do with . . . deeds of darkness, but rather expose them" (Eph 5:11). The biblical response to injustice is not to conceal it or dismiss it offhandedly with phony forgiveness. In Scripture, unrepentant abusers of powerless people incurred appropriate punishment. In contemporary culture, that may involve the legal system.

Connie followed scriptural principles when she took steps to protect her nieces from further physical abuse at the hands of their mother's boyfriend. However, Connie quickly discovered that her biblically correct decision was not popular in her shame-bound family. You may have encountered the same reaction if you've stopped playing "let's-pretend," because this "forgive-forget-and-pretend-it-never-happened" response to genuine childhood pain is the hallmark of shame-based families.

Remember, opening our hearts to authentic forgiveness never requires us to close our eyes to ongoing abuse. And authentic forgiveness never labels deception as "Christian compassion." However, shame-bound families often do both of these things. Clearly, this forgiving business is neither simple nor painless. Since it is such a challenging struggle, why should we even bother?

Why Should We Forgive?

Some people begin to work on forgiving serious hurts after reading a Bible verse, such as Ephesians 4:32, which tells us to forgive others. Since we Christians are forgiven by God and called to relate to him in obedient love, a verse like that may help some of us answer the "why forgive" question.

Others of us need some hope for personal blessing to help sustain us in the arduous forgiving task. While our primary motive should be simply that it's the right thing to do, there are at least two real benefits which we will reap.

1. Forgiving promotes personal well-being. Obeying God always brings blessings. And this is abundantly true with regard to forgiving—it is good for us. That's part of why God tells his forgiven children to forgive. When we give the gift of forgiveness to those who hurt us, we promote our own well-being, whether or not the people who hurt us ever even know we have forgiven them.

Physicians have noted that when we forgive, we allow our bodies to decrease the manufacture of those chemicals which tear us apart, body and soul. When we savor our hatred, our anger and rage, we don't hurt "them," we hurt ourselves. Many physicians' conclusions about body chemistry echo the biblical principle that obeying God brings personal benefits.

2. Forgiving provides a grace-full model. We will never be perfect parents, even if our children were very young, or still *in utero,* when we began to work on being released from shame. This means we will need to confess when we've wronged our children; we'll need to ask them to forgive us. It also means there will be times when we hurt our children without realizing it and, when we are confronted with our legitimate wrongs, we must be willing to admit them and ask for forgiveness.

At those times, we'll face this critical question: will our children forgive us and release us from our past wrongs? Today's forgiveness-*granting* will influence tomorrow's inevitable forgiveness-*seeking,* perhaps more than we want to know. This concept is expressed in what is called "The Adult Child's Golden Rule":

> Live in such a way so that you can expect the same amount of acceptance, love and forgiveness from your children as you showed your parents.[5]

This "Golden Rule" can be a curse when we model unrelenting resentment and bitterness. In Hebrews 12:15, God warns unforgiving Christians about a "root of bitterness" that "defiles" many (NRSV). Surely, our children are some of the "many" we defile when we teach them—by the example of our relationship with our parents—to nurture bitterness and withhold forgiveness.

In *Counseling Adult Children of Alcoholics,* I described a man called Charles who had been deeply hurt by two alcoholic parents. In his bitter unforgiveness, Charles "defiled" his parents for many years with verbal abuse. Unfortunately, Charles could not see that he also was defiling himself and his children by the example he set. The seeds of resentment and unforgiveness Charles sowed with his *parents* grew into a thick root of bitterness that flourished anew as resentment and unforgiveness in his *children*. What Charles had sowed he later reaped as his children turned on him with verbal abuse.

In contrast, adult children from shame-bound families can find this "Golden Rule" a blessing when they model releasing their hurtful parents by forgiving. Even when we must set firm boundaries with unrepentant and denial-entrenched parents, we can exhibit biblical, divinely empowered forgiveness. When we do, our children will be watching . . . and learning how to forgive us.

Clearly, there are several important answers to the "why-should-I-forgive" question. But once we're persuaded that forgiving is worth the hard work it requires, we still face the questions of "who" and "how." Let's consider these two forgiveness questions together as we turn a corner to face the challenge of choosing grace by releasing our parents and ourselves.

How Do We Forgive Our Parents?

"Very carefully!" That was the semi-serious response I once received to the question we're now considering. The other seminar participants giggled and nodded in identification with the respondent's wariness about undertaking the task of forgiving parents.

You may or may not identify with that attitude. In fact, you may not be sure that you even need to deal with this question at all. Here are a few personal signposts that, taken together, point to our need to release our parents by forgiving.

We probably need to forgive when we are

☐ Having clear or vague memories of having been emotionally, physically and/or sexually hurt by our parent(s)

☐ Frequently thinking and/or talking about those hurts

☐ Frequently distracting ourselves from thinking about those hurts with excessive work, sleep and/or food, drugs, church busyness, shopping, and so on

☐ Frequently thinking or dreaming about the injury, misfortune or death of our parent(s)

☐ Consistently avoiding communication with our parent(s) when
we have not confronted the need for appropriate boundaries
☐ Frequently expressing inappropriate and exaggerated anger
☐ Frequently attacking others subtly or blatantly through sarcasm,
personal insults, withholding money or privileges, public humiliation, and so on
☐ Frequently attacking ourselves through excessive self-criticism
☐ Frequently experiencing physical symptoms such as insomnia,
gastrointestinal disorders, muscle tension, and so on
☐ Consistently avoiding communication with God and/or feeling
that God is "out to get me"

Are you convinced you need to forgive your parents? That still
leaves us with "how," doesn't it? My answer is somewhat similar to
the seminar respondent's: *Very realistically.* Our three-part forgiving
formula (face it, feel it, forgive it) provides some direction as we
confront the realities of forgiving our parents for both the past and
the present.

Realities of Forgiving Our Parents
The most effective forgiving seems to require commitment, time,
willingness to endure emotional pain, and a process orientation to the
entire endeavor. It all begins with a willingness to face it.

1. Face it. I've seen many sincere Christians toss out a quick "blanket
forgiveness" in an attempt to cover up and avoid the pain of facing
the past. Blanket forgiving sounds something like, "Oh, Lord, I forgive my parents for everything they ever did that hurt me. Amen."

This quick-fix brand of forgiving looks very spiritual. But it is not
very effective, because it is designed to protect us from the emotional
cost involved in facing specific hurtful acts. Genuine biblical forgiveness deals with specifics and it is costly. That means that forgiveness
takes time—time enough for us to do the necessary groundwork of
facing the specific wrongs and feeling the accompanying emotions.

You may be extremely anxious about delaying forgiveness until you've faced and felt the specific acts being forgiven. If so, you may be more comfortable with consciously and verbally committing to the goal of forgiveness at the very start of your personal recovering process, even though at first you will only be examining and experiencing what needs to be forgiven. If you are working with a professional counselor or lay helper, you might want to write a forgiveness contract clearly articulating your commitment.

Writing is also helpful when you begin to list specific hurts. Making a list provides a structure to guide you in the "face it" step.

Sample Forgiveness List

Parents' Acts

1. Mom called me stupid and clumsy in front of two friends when I was ten.

2. When Dad was drunk, he trapped me in a corner when I was twelve. He rubbed up against me real hard and French-kissed me.

Figure 4-1.

The acts listed in figure 4-1 are adapted from a list written by an adult daughter from a shame-based, dysfunctional family. As you read the descriptions, you may experience unexpectedly strong feelings stirred by empathy and/or familiarity. This raises the reality that forgiving our parents requires feeling what we face.

2. Feel it. Many of us from shame-bound families learned to put our most intense emotions on the back shelf of our internal deep freeze. As we move into recovering and re-viewing, we may notice that our feelings are starting to "thaw." This can be incredibly frightening if we were taught that emotions are dangerous or are signs of weakness. They are neither. They are human, as we will see in more detail in chapter ten.

Because feelings have an amazing ability to escape the boxes we construct to contain them, we need to be very realistic about this "feel it" step. Intense emotions like grief, fear and anger do not dissipate overnight simply because we have identified them as appropriate to childhood hurts. These emotions often wash over us time and time again before they begin to subside. Sometimes we may feel we are being inundated and swept away by them.

If you are frightened by the intensity of the emotions that accompany memories of parental wrongs, please seek some support and guidance from a Christian counselor or some other Christian helper who understands the painful realities of the forgiveness process. Again, the Forgiveness List can help you identify your feelings. In figure 4-2, the "feel it" step has been added. The woman who prepared this list included some of her childhood interpretations of the treatment she received.

Sample Forgiveness List

Parents' Acts	*My Thoughts/Feelings*
1. Mom called me stupid and clumsy in front of two friends when I was ten.	I wanted to die. I felt so ashamed and humiliated. I thought I must really be a worthless person.
2. When Dad was drunk, he trapped me in a corner when I was twelve. He rubbed up against me real hard and French-kissed me.	I felt so dirty and ashamed. I always wondered why he picked me to do that to. I thought maybe he knew something about me that I didn't know about myself.

Figure 4-2.

3. *Forgive it by releasing.* We've already seen that the essence of forgiveness is contained in the concept of releasing, and we've examined giving up the right to retaliate. But there is more for us to release if we want to forgive our parents *realistically* and move into increasingly shame-free living.

Forgiving realistically will undoubtedly shatter our dreams of having the "fantasy family" with totally accepting, loving parents which we crave. We need to release that fantasy and let the dream die. When we do, we'll have to let ourselves honestly grieve the death of that dream. Death-of-the-dream grief is a broader, more global grief than the sadness we feel about specific childhood hurts. And this die-hard dream has more lives than a dozen cats.

How can we tell if we have not yet released the fantasy-family dream? Our expectations will sound something like this when we face family visits. "This time it will be different; this time they'll both stay sober; this time they won't verbally batter each other, me, my spouse or my kids; this time his anger won't ruin the day; this time she will finally accept and love me for who I am; this time . . ."

Unless our parents have sought help for their personal and/or marital problems, it is unrealistic to expect them to be different "this time." Unrealistic expectations explain why we often experience so much fresh hurt and disappointment after family visits.

When we release the fantasy of a better yesterday-family with our parents, we can reach for the reality of a better today-family with our children. However, since our parents are our children's grandparents, we probably will need to release one more fantasy. We may have to grieve the death of the Norman Rockwellish smiling-silver-haired-adoring-and-godly grandparents dream we cherished for our children.

We may struggle with a whole new layer of resentment over this. As one woman in this situation explained, "It's bad enough that I got cheated out of having normal, loving parents. But now my kids are getting cheated out of having normal, loving grandparents. It just breaks my heart when they ask me why my folks don't seem to love them as much as some of their little friends' grandparents. I feel hurt and angry all over again."

As you can see, releasing impaired parents is likely to be a doubly painful process: it may involve both past pain and ongoing pain. Here are two specific suggestions that have proved helpful in moving toward genuine forgiving.

First, study forgiveness. Read about it to correct any lingering misunderstandings you might have. (See appendix C for several book suggestions.) Look up *forgiveness* and *forgive* in a Bible concordance and study the passages listed there.

Second, study your parents. If possible, get photographs of your parents as children and adolescents, and talk to people who knew them when they were young. The more you know about your parents, the more you will understand the forces that shaped them and their choices. Remember, they too are responsible for their adult choices, no matter what happened to them as children. However, seeing our parents as weak and wounded people, like us, will help us move toward forgiving them. Eventually, we must complete the forgiveness preliminaries and come to the point extolled in an advertisement for athletic shoes: "Just do it!"

Again, we can use the Forgiveness List to guide us. Some of my counselees put all of the hurtful childhood facts and feelings in a detailed letter which they read to me and then burn. Others use the "empty chair" method, either in my office or privately. They symbolically seat their parents, then talk to them about their wrongful acts. Whatever the method, we aren't finished until we *explicitly state our choice to forgive.* Remember, releasing by forgiveness is an act of our will—a decision. It is never simply an emotional response of warm, fuzzy feelings for parents or others who have wronged us.

Many people find it helpful to date the decision to forgive and have it witnessed by a counselor, pastor or trusted friend. Figure 4-3 shows the completed samples on the Forgiveness List when this pattern is followed. As you can see from the sample dates, forgiving is usually an ongoing process as new memories surface and as we continue to interact with imperfect and hurtful people.

As challenging as it is to forgive our parents and other important people in our lives, most of us find it even more difficult to forgive ourselves. Yet shame-free living and parenting demands that we choose grace for ourselves too.

Sample Forgiveness List

Parents' Acts	My Thoughts/Feelings	Date Forgiven	Witness
1. Mom called me stupid and clumsy in front of two friends when I was ten.	I wanted to die. I felt so ashamed and humiliated. I thought I must really be a worthless person.	9/21/91	S.D.W
2. When Dad was drunk, he trapped me in a corner when I was twelve. He rubbed up against me real hard and French-kissed me.	I felt so dirty and ashamed. I always wondered why he picked me to do that to. I thought maybe he knew something about me that I didn't know about myself.	4/15/92	S.D.W.

Figure 4-3.

How Do We Forgive Ourselves?

Deep inside, many of us probably believe that if only we had been better children, our parents would have been better parents. This shame-bound perspective of blaming ourselves for others' actions highlights the necessity of approaching self-forgiveness with ruthless realism. This is true especially when we come to our parenting guilt.

In figure 4-4, I contrast examples of genuine guilt (in the parenting realm) that needs to be forgiven with examples of shame-shaped false guilt. Use this chart to help you sort through your parenting guilt bundle to separate reality from fantasy.

Repeated massive doses of truth will eventually cure false guilt. But that still leaves us with severe symptoms of genuine guilt and the fatal disease underlying it. The Bible calls that disease sin.

Scripture clearly and repeatedly states that all people have sinned. We readily recognize the biblical truth that parents sin in ways that cause suffering for their children. (See Ex 20:5.) That's why we need to forgive. On the other hand, the Bible also teaches that children eventually must be accountable for their own sinful choices. (See Ezek 18:20.) That's why we need to be forgiven.

Examples of False and True Parenting Guilt

False Parenting Guilt	*True Parenting Guilt*
1. Not following my parents' "rules" for parenting	1. Causing "fetal alcohol syndrome" in my child because of my alcohol abuse
2. Not being able to "fix" my parents so they can be good grandparents	2. Publicly humiliating my child by loud, sarcastic comments and ridicule
3. Not being a perfect parent	3. Failing to protect my child from spouse's physical abuse to avoid spouse's anger
4. Not automatically knowing all about child development	4. Allowing my child to ride with an intoxicated grandparent to "keep peace"

Figure 4-4.

Because of his gracious love, God provided the sin cure for all sinful parents and children in the person of Jesus Christ. When we agree with God that we need a Savior from sin, and when we accept Jesus' death as the payment for our sin, God declares us forgiven, released from sin's penalty and reconciled to him as his dear children. We really have no basis for forgiving ourselves until we have received forgiveness from God. But once we have been forgiven by God, we have no basis for *not* forgiving ourselves. When we fail to choose grace and to release ourselves (as God has done for us), we mock the adequacy of Jesus' death on the cross and God's promise to forgive.

It is one thing to be able to quote 1 John 1:7, "the blood of Jesus his Son purifies us from all sin." It is another thing to appropriate that truth for yourself. Read that verse again and let its liberating message saturate your grace-thirsty soul and ease your guilt-laden heart. You know that God is not a liar. And he did not include that verse just to make the type come out even on that page of the Bible. What's more, "all sin" means *all* sin—even our worst *parenting* sins.

When we can acknowledge our wrongs, "come clean" and be real with God, we will be well on the way to being able to acknowledge our wrongs, "come clean" and be real with others, including our children.

Seeking Our Children's Forgiveness

We've already considered the personal benefits of providing a grace-full model of forgiveness to our children by forgiving our parents. And when we sincerely acknowledge our parenting wrongs and ask for forgiveness, we make it easier for our children to release us. I know this is true, because I have experienced the reality of children's eagerness to forgive their repentant parents.

I have asked my children to forgive me for the times I failed to parent them lovingly and wisely. They both have been lavish and loving in their outpouring of forgiveness. As an example, here is part of the note that Dave, at age thirty, wrote in my 1991 Mother's Day card.

> Mom, it is important to me that you realize that I look back on my growing-up years with *very* fond memories. I *never* doubted I was loved. I always knew you were interested in hearing about my feelings. And unlike most kids, as I grow older I have grown to respect, admire and love you more and more. . . .

As you've probably guessed, I wept with a mixture of joy, relief and awe at my adult son's willingness to choose grace by releasing and forgiving his painfully imperfect mother. I was thankful that I had shared with Dave and Becky my struggle to sincerely forgive my mother. And I was thankful they both know the reality of God's grace which empowered Dave's choice to grace me with forgiveness.

Remember, if our parents are still bound by the shame lie, they feel uniquely, hopelessly subhuman when they make mistakes. Whether or not our parents ever escape the intergenerational shame-cycle, choose truth, acknowledge their wrongs and ask us for forgiveness, *we can do that with our children.* And when we do, we begin a new, intergenerational *grace*-cycle.

As I write this chapter, Dave and his precious wife, Dru, are expecting their first child (our first grandchild) within a few weeks. Dave has already demonstrated his willingness and capacity to choose grace by releasing his imperfect parents through forgiveness. I confidently expect Dave's children will follow his grace-full pattern when it is their turn to forgive him.

Personal Reflection

1. Have you ever explicitly sought God's forgiveness by asking Jesus to come into your life? You can do that right this moment by praying something like this: *Dear Jesus, I believe that you died for my sins and I accept you as my personal Savior. Please come into my life, be my Lord and make me all you want me to be. Thank you for promising that you would. Amen.*

☐ If you do not already attend a church that demonstrates God's grace and love, please find one as soon as possible. Get into a Bible study and find a more experienced Christian (of the same sex) who can encourage and support you as you grow in your faith.

2. Having experienced God's forgiveness, are you willing to begin a "Forgiveness List" of your parents' hurtful actions?

☐ If so, when?

☐ If not, what would it take to make you willing?

3. Are you willing to learn more about your parents to facilitate your forgiving?

☐ If so, what's your first step?

☐ If not, will you ask God to make you "willing to be willing"?

4. Do you need to ask your children to forgive you? (You will not "lose face." You will gain respect.)

☐ Since you are not a perfect parent, I am assuming you *do* need to ask. When will you do it?

Looking Ahead

The next chapter focuses on what we didn't learn when we were children in shame-based families. Instead of feeling an enormous surge of shame at the idea of not knowing, let's recognize that nobody is born automatically knowing how to be a wise and loving parent. Then we will tackle some specific growth areas.

5
We Can Learn What We Don't Know

*S*cratch most parents and we bleed guilt.

And if we are parents who grew up in very unhealthy families, we fairly hemorrhage with shame because we don't automatically know everything there is to know about how to be (almost) perfect parents. Furthermore, we have this uneasy feeling that our children want us to be almost perfect.

Then, to make matters worse, we come across articles like the one I recently read about the responses of 21,000 nine- and ten-year-olds to the question of who was their greatest hero. Whom do you think they picked: (a) Bart Simpson; (b) President Bush; (c) Paula Abdul; (d) Bo Jackson; or (e) none of the above? The answer is (e), because those fourth-graders overwhelmingly named their parents as their greatest heroes. The article's author concluded that "children are looking for role models, and they are looking close to home. . . . It seems to me that our children are telling us loud and clear: Please act like the role models we want you to be."[1]

We didn't need that added pressure, did we? When it comes to parenting, most of us already feel it's like being required to perform brain surgery in a dark room at midnight—blindfolded! We suspect there's a lot of critical information we don't know, and we don't even know what we don't know.

But we can learn. That's the hopeful finding of a recent University of Rochester program where nurses taught disadvantaged mothers how to play and talk with their children. Only four per cent of these mothers neglected or abused their children, compared with nineteen per cent of those who received no training. Even mothers who had been abused as children learned how to be nurturing parents.[2]

To become increasingly shame-free people and parents, we need to focus on three major areas of learning: family dynamics, basics of child development and recognition of our own parenting styles. These three learning areas obviously affect our parenting, and they encompass most of what many of us don't know.

Learning About Healthy Family Dynamics

Jack and Judith Balswick offer the following observations about healthy, biblical family dynamics and parenting ideals.

1. Parent/child relationships begin when the parents make a one-way unconditional commitment of love (a unilateral covenant) with their child. This means that in healthy families children don't have to earn their parents' love; it is a gift. (The term "earned gift" is self-contradicting.)

2. Ideally, as the child matures this initial covenant matures into a *two-way* unconditional commitment of love between parents and child. The child learns to love the parents in response to the parents' love.

3. This two-way love commitment establishes an environment of

grace and forgiveness where there is substantially shame-free, mutual knowing and caring between parents and child.

4. Wise, biblical parents empower their children to become competent and capable people who will, in turn, empower others. (This process is similar to Jesus' relationship with his disciples.)

"Parental empowering is the affirmation of the child's ability to learn, grow, and become all that one is meant to be as part of God's image and creative plan. . . . The most effective [parental] empowerers are those individuals who have themselves been empowered by the unconditional love of God."[3]

Let's compare this to banking. We must have something in our personal "caring-and-competence-accounts" in order to "deposit" caring and competence in our children's personal "accounts." Healthy, wise (but imperfect) parents consistently deposit substantial sums of love, affirmation, encouragement, skill training, discipline, comfort and biblical values in their children's personal accounts. When the children mature, they draw upon these deposits to face the challenges of adult life, and they invest deposits in the lives of others, especially their own children. But if we enter adulthood shame-bound and near "personhood bankruptcy," we have few personal, emotional or spiritual "nest eggs" with which to handle life's inevitable "rainy days." And we have little or nothing extra to invest in our children.

You may fear that you are teetering on the edge of "personhood bankruptcy" and have been unable to make substantial caring and competence deposits in your children. Remember, this chapter promises that you can learn how to do what you don't know how to do—and God will empower you in the process.

My friend Cathy knows that's true. "My mom never taught me to cook, so my poor husband and little girl get the results of my on-the-job training in the kitchen," Cathy told me. "It would be easier to keep my three-year-old out of the kitchen instead of letting her 'help.' My mom never let me near the kitchen when she was cooking because she said I was too messy. But my daughter is so eager to learn

Overview of Child and Parent Development

	Child's Part	Parent's Parts		
	Child's Task	*Helpful Responses*	*Unhelpful Responses*	*Affirmations*
STAGE ONE: Birth to 6 Months	Call for care by crying or fussing; accept touch and nurture; cuddle and coo; emotionally bond, learn to trust caring adults and self.	Give loving, consistent care; respond to baby's needs; think for baby; hold and look at baby while feeding; nurture by touching, talking, singing. Be reliable and trustworthy; get help when unsure how to care for baby; commit child daily to God's care; *nurture selves and each other.*	Unresponsive to baby's signaling; not touching and holding enough; agitated, angry or rigid responses; feeding before the baby signals; unsafe physical environment; lack of protection; criticizing or punishing; discounting.	We're glad you are here with us. You belong here. What you need is important. You can grow at your own pace. We are glad you are you. We love you and we care for you willingly. *(You are affirming the child for being.)*
STAGE TWO: 6 to 18 Months	*Continue tasks from Stage One.*	*Continue to offer cuddling, love, safety and protection, and to commit child to God.*		*Affirm for doing.*
	Develop sensory awareness by using all senses to explore environment; continue forming secure attachments with parents; start to learn that all problems are not easily solved; get help in times of stress; develop initiative; start using words during middle or latter part of stage; learn more about God's love.	Continue nurturing touch; encourage; say two "yeses" for every "no"; provide variety of safe experiences for child; listen and avoid interrupting child when possible; talk to child about God's love; read children's Bible stories and other books to child; *take care of own needs.*	Restricting mobility; shaming child for exploring; failing to protect; expecting child not to touch "precious" objects; punishing the child for exploring; expecting toilet training; ridiculing child's attempts to use words.	You can experiment and explore with all your senses. We will keep you safe. You can do things as many times as you need. You can feel all your feelings. You can know what you know. You can be interested in everything. We love you when you are quiet and when you are active.

STAGE THREE: 18 Months to 3 Years

Continue tasks from earlier stages.

Continue to offer cuddling, love, safety and protection, and to commit child to God.

Affirm for thinking.

Learn to think for self; solve problems, understand cause and effect; start to follow simple commands; learn to express anger (without hurting others) and other feelings; separate from parents without losing their love; start to give up belief about being the center of the universe; learn more about God's love, wisdom and power; learn to pray.	Affirm child's thinking ability; encourage cause and effect thinking; provide reasons, how to's; accept all feelings; teach options instead of hitting or biting. Set and enforce reasonable limits; remain constant in face of child's outbursts; give clear directions child can follow; encourage and praise achievement; expect child to think about own feelings and start to think about others' feelings; refer to child as a "terrific two"; teach child to see God's care and protection in daily life; teach child to pray; *take care of own needs.*	Too many "don'ts" and not enough "do's"; referring to child as a "terrible two"; trying to look like perfect parents by having always compliant child; expecting child to play "with" before learning to play "near" others; not setting limits; not expecting child to think for self; shaming by expecting more than child can do developmentally, e.g., sitting still throughout worship service.	We're glad you are thinking for yourself. It's okay to be angry; we won't let you hurt yourself or others. You can push and test our limits as much as you need to and we will not take away our limits or our love. You can think and feel at the same time. You can know what you need and ask for help. You can separate from us and we will continue to love you.

STAGE FOUR: 3 to 6 Years

Continue tasks from earlier stages.

Continue to offer cuddling, love, safety and protection, and to commit child to God.

Affirm for identity and competence.

Assert identity as separate from others; learn about self, own body, sex role, one's effect on others, place in groups; learn that behaviors have consequences; practice appropriate social behavior; separate fantasy from reality; learn what does and does not have power to control; learn more about God and his love.	Support as child continues to explore the world of people, things, ideas, feelings; encourage child to enjoy being a boy or girl; teach that both sexes are great; answer questions truthfully, provide correct information about environment, human body, sex, etc.; provide appropriate positive or negative consequences for actions; compliment appropriate behavior.	Ridiculing; teasing; inconsistency; not expecting child to think for self; unwillingness to answer questions truthfully; use of fantasy to frighten or confuse; responding to child's fantasy as if real; ridiculing for role playing or fantasies; expecting child to care for younger siblings; discounting, i.e., treating child as less valuable than he/she truly is.	You can explore who you and others are; you can be powerful and ask for help at the same time; you can learn the results of your behavior; you can learn what is pretend and what is real; all your feelings are okay with us. We love who you are. God loves you.

Figure 5-1.

to cook—and I am determined to teach her, so we're learning togeth-er." Cathy also made the effort to learn about family dynamics by participating in a group offered at her church.

Cathy and the group learned that one of the most common dy-namics in unhealthy families involves the unrealistic expectations impaired parents have for their children. Of course, as we've noted before, if we grew up in these families we didn't realize our parents' expectations were unrealistic; they were just *there.* Therefore, the most natural thing is to automatically dump all those unrealistic expecta-tions on our children, who, like us years before, will learn to feel subhuman and shame-full because they cannot possibly fulfill them.

But the good news is that we can change that shame-bound pat-tern by learning about how children develop.

Learning About Child Development

"Act your age!" Did your folks ever yell that at you? Have you ever repeated that demand to your children? The question is, how will we or our folks know whether children are acting their ages unless we and they know something about child development?

As a start, figure 5-1 gives an overview of children's major devel-opmental tasks from birth to six years of age. As you will see, at each of the child's developmental stages there are reciprocal developmental responses for parents. I've included some helpful and unhelpful pa-rental responses along with some suggested affirmations.[4]

Another part of the parental learning process includes evaluating our own parenting styles so that we can recognize and build upon the positive aspects while minimizing the unhelpful ones.

Learning About Our Parenting Styles

As we saw in figure 5-1, parenting tasks change as our children grow and change. It is not only appropriate but absolutely essential that parents think for their infants. However, it is inappropriate and de-cidedly unhelpful if we are still doing all of our first-grader's thinking. This means our parenting styles must be flexible and responsive to our children's developmental changes.

Parenting styles can be seen as progressing through four developmental stages, listed by the Balswicks, which correspond to our children's levels of maturity.[5]

1. *Telling:* This style is needed when children are very young and unable to do things on their own. It is characterized by one-way communication: parents tell their children what to do; parents exercise a very high level of control.

2. *Teaching:* For children with low to moderate maturity, this style works best. Although there are dialog and discussion, most of the communication is still done by parents as they answer questions and show children how to do age-appropriate tasks.

3. *Participating:* As they engage in activities with their moderately to highly mature children, parents function more as "player-coaches" who exercise less control with this style. Parents encourage their children to begin doing things their own ways and allow their children to learn through trial and error. Parents continue to provide support, encouragement and consolation when needed.

4. *Delegating:* For very mature, responsible children, this is the parenting style of choice. Parents don't need to exercise much, if any, control because their children are both able and willing to take responsibility and perform tasks on their own. In fact, mature children may interpret their parents' continued high levels of control and support as a sign that their parents lack confidence in them.

Did you identify your current parenting style? Does it correspond appropriately to your children's maturity levels? Of course there are other ways to identify our parenting patterns. For example, if we select one parent-child interaction, set in one moment in time, we may be able to recognize our child-care styles.

Figure 5-2 displays such a comparison of parental caregiving styles in response to a hypothetical childhood injury. As you will see, four styles are shame-based to one degree or another. Only the "assertive"

Comparison of Parental Caregiving Styles[6]
Situation: School-Age Child Has a Badly Scraped Arm.

		Characteristic of Style	*Example of Style*
Shame-Bound Styles	**Active Abandonment**	Relating to child by assault, by physical or psychological invasion that sends direct or indirect "don't be" messages. "Active Abandonment" negates the child's needs with abuse.	Parent doesn't care for wounds. Says something like, "Stop that sniffling or I'll give you something to *really* cry about." Parent yells at and/or shakes the child.
	Passive Abandonment	"Passive Abandoning" is neglect or passive abuse with lack of emotional or physical attention by parents who are unavailable or who ignore the child's needs. These parents may be "there, but not *really* there."	Parent ignores the scrape because parent is uninterested or distracted or, perhaps, intoxicated. Or parent says something like "Don't bother me," because parent is "too busy" or uninterested.
	Measuring	The care a "Measuring" parent gives child is based on parent's needs and expectations, not on the child's needs. Parents who use this conditional care connect with the child by use of threats and conditions.	Parent says something like, "If you don't stop all that fussing, I won't bandage your arm, you crybaby."
	Marshmallowing	"Marshmallowing" is an indulgent, "sticky," patronizing kind of love that promotes the child's continuing dependence on parents who teach child *not* to think for self and *not* to be responsible *for* self or *to* others.	Parent rushes to child and says something like, "Oh, look at your arm, you poor little thing. That really stings! I'll bandage it. Go lie down in front of the TV and I'll do all your chores for you."
Shame-Free Styles	**Assertive**	"Assertive Care" is comforting, loving and freely given by parent. It is helpful to the child, responsive to the child's needs and appropriate to the circumstances.	Parent gives loving care and a hug. Cleans and dresses wound. Parent says something like, "Your arm is scraped! I'm sorry."
	Supportive	Nurturing "Supportive Care" offers help, comfort and love. It encourages the child to think and to do what he/she is capable of doing for himself/herself.	(Because child is mature enough, parent has already taught child how to clean a scrape.) So, parent says (in a concerned and loving tone) something like, "I see you've scraped your arm. Does it hurt? Do you want to take care of it, or would you like some help from me?" Offers a hug.

Figure 5-2.

and "supportive" styles reflect healthy, biblical, shame-free views of parental child-care rooted in respectful, biblical, shame-free views of human beings (even the youngest ones).

Clearly, both of these charts are more representative than exhaustive. We see enough, however, to realize that we *can* learn now what we didn't learn about substantially shame-free families and parenting when we were growing up.

Personal Reflection

☐ Have you struggled with false guilt about not knowing automatically—magically—how to be a nearly perfect parent after growing up with consistently inadequate parents?

☐ Can you see that this expectation was unrealistic and shame-based? ("There is something uniquely wrong with me that isn't wrong with anybody else in the world because I wasn't born knowing how to be a nearly perfect parent.")

☐ Can you identify your parenting style?

☐ If so, are you disheartened or encouraged? Remember, *you can learn to be a better parent.* Read good books on the subject. See appendix C for some suggestions to get you started. Watching and talking to healthier parents is another way to learn. Most important, remember that we can seek wisdom from our heavenly Parent who loves us and never shames us.

Looking Ahead

Growing up in shame-bound families, we developed a lot of distorted thinking, including distorted concepts of God. In chapters four and five, I have recommended that we release our parents and our pasts and commit ourselves and our children into the hands of God. We will never do that unless we trust him, and we will never trust him until we correct our distorted concepts and learn to know God as he really is.

Then when *we* learn, we can teach our children.

6
We Can Learn and Teach About God

*P*arents are powerfully persuasive theologians.

Consider this evidence: A journalist once asked a renowned theologian and author of many massive theological texts how he knew that all he wrote about God was true. The learned professor replied, "My mother told me it was."[1]

Some of us may have grown up singing, "Jesus loves me, this I know for the Bible tells me so." But on some deeper level all of us might as well have sung, "God is (blank blank), this I know for my mom and dad told me so." And of course, how we fill in the blanks makes all the difference.

God is _____ . If I asked you to complete this statement, what would you say? Many of us might be surprised—even shocked—if we stopped to honestly assess our concepts of God. Gloria was.

"How in the world am I going to teach Sarah to love God when I've always been terrified of him?" asked Gloria, a young mother. She continued wistfully, "At church, they tell us that parents are primarily responsible for teaching their kids about God. I believe that, but I'm not sure I really know what God is like. In fact, the only thing I know for sure is that I don't want my little girl to learn what *I* did from *my* folks."

Gloria's church is correct. The Bible instructs parents to teach their children about God and his ways. For example, Psalm 78:2-7 says:

I will utter hidden things, things from of old—what we have heard and known, what our fathers have told us. We will not hide them from their children; we will tell the next generation the praiseworthy deeds of the LORD, his power, and the wonders he has done. He decreed statutes . . . and established the law . . . which he commanded our forefathers to teach their children, so the next generation would know them, even the children yet to be born, and they in turn would tell their children. Then they would put their trust in God and would not forget his deeds.

From this passage and others, we see that when it comes to spiritual/religious matters, God has a two-part plan for parents: to know him personally and to teach their children about him and his ways so that they will seek to know him personally and, in turn, teach *their* children.

But there's a problem with this plan if parents fail to teach accurately about God and his ways. We discover the tragic results in Judges 2:10-12: "another generation grew up, who knew neither the LORD nor what he had done."

To some degree, we are all heirs of that untaught generation if we grew up in unhealthy families, whether they were nonreligious or churchgoing. I mean that many of us do not really know who God is or what he has done. How tragic this is when we consider that God *wants* us to know him so that we will trust him. (See Ps 9:10.)

God is not playing cosmic hide-and-seek by receding into a galactic "black hole" yelling, "Catch me if you can." Psalm 9:16 declares, "The LORD has made himself known" (NRSV). God makes himself generally knowable through his creation (Rom 1:20). But he reveals himself specifically in the Scriptures and supremely in Jesus Christ. And Jesus proclaimed the good news that, through faith in him, we can know God accurately and personally (Jn 1:18; 14:9).

This was indeed good news to Gloria when she heard it. And it can be good news to all the rest of us who need to learn what God is *really* like so that we can teach our children.

With the promise of Jesus' good news in mind, let's begin this learning and teaching enterprise by exploring our current God-concepts and how we acquired them.

God of Our Fathers

It has become virtually a cliché to say that *we* make God in *our* image, or more specifically, in the image of our parents—especially our *fathers*. Over and over I see this confirmed in my life and the lives of other believers.

Stated simply: *My parents'(especially my father's) treatment of me has profoundly shaped the concept of God that underlies my personal relationship with God.* If this premise is true, we should be able to see evidence of that connection. The following exercise may help provide some evidence.

On a piece of paper or in your personal journal, write brief answers to the following questions about your father or the person who functioned in the father-role for you.

1. How close were you to your father—that is, how approachable was your father?

2. Did he show you that you were intrinsically valuable and unconditionally loved, or did you have to perform to earn value and love?

3. Did he have time for you—that is, were you important enough to him to get his (appropriate) attention? (Sometimes, when fathers/parents spend time with their children, it is inappropriate and hurt-

ful. For example, it is inappropriate for your father to spend time with you for his sexual gratification or as an excuse to get out of the house so he can drink.)

4. Did he keep his promises (was he trustworthy)?

5. Were you punished for being bad or disciplined for character improvement?

Now on a separate page, answer the same questions about God. For example, "How close am I to God—that is, how approachable is he?" When you finish answering the second set of questions, compare your responses to the two sets.[2]

Did you discover any similarities? That's not bad news for those adults who had basically well-functioning parents who were consistently approachable, loving and trustworthy. However, to one degree or another, most of us raised in less healthy families have learned some unbiblical concepts of God.

As you attempt to assess your own view of God, see if you can recognize one or more of these *"distorted deities"* that I have identified from my clinical experience and my personal life.

The Dangerous God
Sonja is a lovely Christian woman who feels panicky when she thinks about bowing prostrate—face to the floor—before God, as Scripture describes. She is terrified at the thought of being in such a powerless position in front of God. Why? This is how she explained it.

"I just feel like I have to keep both eyes open and stay prepared because somehow God seems dangerous to me. I mean he will hurt me if I don't try to do everything just right and stay really alert!"

This "dangerous deity" is cruel to the core. He whimsically elects to flex his sovereign muscles by zapping his hapless creatures with catastrophes.

Sonja's spiritual struggle made sense when she began to remember that her alcoholic father frequently sodomized her for punishment when she was a little girl. These brutal "special spankings" left Sonja believing that, when she makes mistakes, she deserves and will eventually experience excruciatingly painful punishment because God, as a father, is cruel and extremely dangerous.

Sonja is just one of the thousands of sincere and struggling Christians who have been spiritually abused by fathers/parents who, as caregivers, profoundly misrepresented the character of God.

These people are left with a contradiction. They are told that God is a loving Father. Well, they can grasp the concept of "loving." And they understand the meaning of "father." But because of the abuse they received from their own fathers, putting those two concepts together seems like a contradiction in terms.

The Demanding God

I know only a few people who have been as profoundly abused as Sonja and have learned to see God as dangerous. But many more of us view God as terribly demanding.

This distorted deity also carries a big stick—a *measuring* stick. And if this is our concept of God, we may see him as a scowling taskmaster who is never satisfied no matter how hard we try to please him. That's how Paul felt as he told me:

> For as long as I can remember, I have seen God as disappointed and angry with me. He was always up in heaven, standing with his arms crossed over his chest, slowly shaking his head and scowling. God was looking down at me and saying, "Paul, Paul, Paul, I am so disappointed in you. I expected so much more of you. Now here is your new list of rules; get out there and do better."
> . . . I always feel that I should be doing more to please God. I never do enough.[3]

If we worship this demanding deity, we tend to feel that he not only jerks his measuring stick higher after each of our spiritual pole vaults—he never really forgives when we inevitably fall short.

When I first assessed my own God-concept a few years ago, I

realized that, like Paul, I worshiped a demanding deity who expected more from me than from his other children. Curiously, my misperceptions about God sprang from my mother's attempt to impress me with the fact that I was "special."

In retrospect, I think Mother was trying to show me that, although I didn't have an *earthly* father to love me, my *heavenly* Father loved me and had proved it by giving me some "gifts," such as playing the piano and singing, memorizing easily and getting good grades. I believe she did this because she loved me and deeply regretted my father-loss, but also because her painfully poor self-concept was salved to think that she had given birth to a "special" child.

Consequently, average was intolerable and extraordinary was my minimum daily requirement. A major accomplishment might have been a big deal for some *other* child, but not for *me* because God had given me "gifts." And I nearly strangled on the strings my sincerely loving mother attached to those gifts.

As is frequently the case with Christian parents, my mother used scriptural support for her perfectionistic expectations of me. I can still hear her quoting the portion of Luke 12:48 that says, "From everyone who has been given much, much will be demanded."

My perception of this verse stirred a sense of gratitude for being "given much," while it generated guilt because so much *more* always seemed to be required no matter how much I did. As a result, I grew up loving both God and my mother because they had given me so much. Yet simultaneously, I feared that both God and my mother were constantly disappointed in me because I could never *fully* satisfy their demands.

The Discriminating God

I've noticed a curious phenomenon among many sincerely devout Christians. They would never say that God is dangerously cruel or demanding and unforgiving with his children—his *other* children. But they experience God as selectively unfair with them despite Scripture's saying otherwise (Acts 10:34).

Zach was raised by a harsh father and a mother who favored her daughters. His comment when asked to describe God was, "God plays favorites." He explained, "I have always felt more like God's *step*child than an honest to goodness born-into-his-family child. Somehow, I don't seem to know how to have the close, loving communication with God that other Christians seem to have. They get gifts from God, but I just get the back of his hand."

Zach feels that God overlooks him while showering attention on other believers. This "I-am-worth-less-to-God" feeling reveals the perceptual scars from Zach's shame-based childhood, which was characterized by neglect from consistently impaired parents.

The Disinterested God

There's yet another distorted deity, one who does not shower anything on anybody. He is too distant and uninterested. I've met many Christians who hold this misperception of God. Some of them still believe that God loves them; however, most of them also believe that he doesn't get personally involved in our lives today.

"He is way out *there*—but not right *here*," Carolyn sighed, as the adult Sunday-school class discussed concepts of God. Carolyn is like many Christians who were not wounded by hands-on violence, yet carry the scars of spiritual abuse in their lives. She discovered this after several months of counseling with her pastor. Carolyn sheepishly confessed that, for as long as she could remember, she had despised saying "the Lord's Prayer."

"Suddenly last Sunday, as we were coming to the part of the service where everyone says the Lord's Prayer, I felt myself tensing up," Carolyn explained. "I felt anxious and full of self-hatred. Then I realized that that was exactly how I felt as a kid every time I had to go to my dad to ask for something or even try to talk about anything. He never really listened or talked to me. He just seemed too busy or bored. So I learned to avoid communicating with my father about anything."

Initially, Carolyn's pastor was shocked by her comments. He knew that she came from a "devout churchgoing family." Like many of us, this pastor had assumed that regularly going to the Father's *house* means really knowing the Father's *heart.* It doesn't.

Father or Pharisee?

The Pharisees of Jesus' day were the Jewish leaders who taught that real godliness consisted primarily of keeping rigid rules governing every area of life. These religionists elevated "appearance management" to a fine art. They feared and hated Jesus because he exposed their preoccupation with externals by ripping off their masks of righteousness to reveal hearts of "hypocrisy and wickedness." (See Mt 23:25-28.)

Sadly, appearance management with its emphasis on the externals—how we *look* rather than how we *are*—is alive and well in many "religious" homes today. And if we were raised in homes like that, we learned to see God as the "heavenly Pharisee." This caricature of our heavenly Father seems most concerned about how often we attend church (and what translation of the Bible we carry and how long our hair and hems are). When we fail to fulfill his lengthy list of religious regulation, this "heavenly Pharisee" loves us less. He may even throw us out of his family.

However, everything will be spiritually satisfactory with this heavenly Pharisee as long as we attend all the church services and activities. To be *super*-spiritual we have to do that *and* hold as many church leadership positions as possible. And if we seek *saintly* super-spirituality, we need to do all of the above plus hold denominational leadership positions and/or go to the mission field!

When you stop to think about it, this heavenly-Pharisee-god is perfectly suited to the needs of impaired and abusive parents who teach secret-keeping to protect themselves and their dysfunctional families' public images. Conveniently, this heavenly Pharisee doesn't seem to care very much about what goes on in our homes—or in our hearts.

As improbable as it may seem, some parents who neglect or abuse their children attend church faithfully and even hold church and denominational leadership positions. I cringe when I remember the many times I've heard Christian women (and men) describe sexual abuse from their fathers, grandfathers, uncles or other family members who were pastors, missionaries or leaders in denominational or parachurch organizations.

Sometimes these "religious" abuse perpetrators quote Bible verses lifted from context and twisted to justify their sins. Ephesians 6:1, "Children, obey your parents in the Lord, for this is right," is one of their favorites. These adults conveniently overlook the verses that admonish parents, specifically fathers, to avoid causing their children to become embittered and discouraged. (See Col 3:21; Eph 6:4.) These Bible-quoting parents deeply wound their children with spiritual abuse that creates enormous barriers to knowing and trusting God—and for good reason. *These parents have represented God to their children as the co-perpetrator of their abuse!* In effect these parents are saying, "God approves of what we are doing to you, and here's the verse to prove it."

Clearly, most Christian parents do not victimize their children with hands-on abuse. Nevertheless, whenever well-meaning but misled parents teach the heavenly-Pharisee concept of God, they are spiritually abusing their children. And this can happen even when the parents *talk* about grace. That's what created Vic's spiritual confusion.

Vic was in a seminary class I taught. He spoke openly about the theological contradiction he had battled throughout his training for ministry.

"I can remember hearing about God's grace at church and in our daily 'family altar,' but my concept of grace was distorted because my parents lived under 'law' instead," Vic told me. He described his upper-middle-class family as one in which his parents set extraordinarily low limits on what could be spent for birthday and Christmas gifts—and then they attached strings even to those. "As every birthday or Christmas got near, my folks would keep reminding me that I'd better behave if I expected to deserve a gift."

In such a climate, Vic never really understood the concept of God's "free gift" of salvation spoken of in Ephesians 2:8. Consequently, concluding that neither his folks nor even God meant what they said when they talked of grace as being free and undeserved, Vic viewed God's grace from the contradictory perspective of "earned gift."

Here's how Vic summarized it: "They *talked* grace but they *walked* law, works, and 'strings attached.' I concluded pretty early that my folks and God really didn't mean what they said when they talked about grace being free."

Maybe you also have been spiritually wounded by your well-intentioned Christian parents. Remember, they probably taught you what they had been taught about God by *their* well-intentioned parents. But we don't have to continue that pattern.

Since you have read this far, no doubt you are committed to changing your distorted concepts of God because you want to teach your children about God more accurately. So far, we've learned that God is not like our dysfunctional parents and he is not a heavenly *Pharisee*. Now what we need is someone who will show us the what the heavenly *Father* is like. As always, God has perfectly anticipated and met our need.

"Show Us the Father"

"Lord, show us the Father and that will be enough for us," cried Philip the night before Jesus died. Healing for distorted God-concepts and spiritual abuse wounds still flows from Jesus' awesome answer: "Anyone who has seen me has seen the Father" (Jn 14:9).

The key to transforming our relationship with God is not mastering a program. It is meeting a Person—Jesus Christ.

Jesus is God "with skin on." This means that when we want to know how God relates to people in various circumstances, we can find out by learning from Scripture how Jesus did it.

However, I know some Christians who aren't so sure about that.

Laura is one of those Christians who are not convinced that Jesus accurately reflects the character of God the Father. "Oh, I know that in my head," she said, tapping her right temple. "But it doesn't seem to make the trip down to my heart. Besides, Jesus seems so much nicer than the God of the Old Testament. I'm embarrassed to admit it, but it's almost as if Jesus is a 'kinder, gentler God' designed by George Bush's speech writers!"

You may be as surprised as Laura to learn that "the God of the Old Testament" is described as being like a comforting, nurturing mother as well as a strong, wise father. In Isaiah 66:13 God promises, "As a mother comforts her child, so will I comfort you." And God says that even if a nursing mother might forget her infant—a pretty unlikely situation—he will never forget us (see Is 49:15-16).

Even when God is referred to as a father in the Old Testament, he is seen as more tender than tough. For example, in Psalm 103:13-14 God is described as having fatherly compassion and great understanding. And for those of us who know the indescribable pain of father-loss through divorce, desertion or death, God promises to be "a father to the fatherless" (see Ps 68:5).

As I write this chapter, Dabney, our first grandchild, is four weeks old. I am looking at a photograph of our son, sitting in a rocker while his infant daughter sleeps peacefully on his big chest. Dave is a six-foot-two Olympic medalist and a successful professional. And, having just returned from a week's visit with Dabney and her folks, I saw that Dave also is a comforting, nurturing, gentle daddy who is keenly aware of his awesome responsibility to represent God to his child. My granddaughter will be able to reconcile the tenderness and strengths of our Father-God and recognize him in Jesus more easily than many of us; she has a dad who exhibits those qualities.

Unfortunately, most of us did not have dads like that. Yet, almost without exception, I have found that even people with ghastly memories of their fathers can learn to love and trust Jesus.

Jesus is both the finish line in our journey to *know* about God "as he really is" and the starting block in our desire to *teach* about God "as he really is." This is no surprise, considering that Hebrews 12:2 describes Jesus as "the author and finisher" or "the pioneer and perfecter" of our faith (depending on the translation).

So as we turn a corner from learning about God to teaching our children about God, Jesus retains the spotlight.

Teaching Younger Children: Right from the Start

Children can understand and respond to Jesus' love and trustworthiness long before they can grasp the concept of the invisible heavenly Father. Here are a few suggestion to help our younger children fall in love with Jesus from the start.[4]

1. As soon as your baby can sit long enough, use "Jesus books" with lots of colorful pictures to talk about. You can do this many months before your child will want you to read from Bible storybooks.

2. Throughout the day, sing "Jesus songs" and use child-oriented "Jesus music" tapes and records. If you don't know any, ask a Christian friend or check your Christian bookstore for suggestions.

3. Pray child-sized prayers *frequently*—not just at meals and bedtime. We most effectively teach that prayer is "talking to Jesus" when our children hear us doing it naturally and regularly throughout the day. This helps your child know that Jesus is very real to you.

4. Choose a picture of Jesus, preferably one with young children, for your child's room. Talk about Jesus' love for children.

5. When your child is a little older, bedtime "visits with Jesus" can incorporate Bible stories and prayers. This becomes a precious time for both parents and children.

6. Look for ways to connect truths about God to your child's experiences. For example, one father was walking with his children in

the woods when he spotted a chipmunk. He explained that God loved that little animal enough to give it protective coloring. He concluded his impromptu theology lesson by emphasizing that if God cares that much for chipmunks, we can be sure that he will care for us.

I know another father who purposefully chose to model God's grace by shortening his daughter's "grounding" so she could attend a long-anticipated party. He also took the time to explain why he was doing it. Remember, in 2 Peter 3:18 God urges us to "grow in the grace and knowledge of our Lord and Savior Jesus Christ." Sometimes we put all our effort into increasing our children's *knowledge* about Jesus but neglect to model and teach about his *grace*.

7. Psalm 107 (NRSV) encourages God's redeemed people to "say so." As our children get old enough to understand, one of the most spiritually helpful things we can do is to tell them about the many times God has shown his loving care in our lives. At the same time, we can teach them how to spot these times in their own lives and how to "say so."

8. Find a healthy church family where you and your children can learn about God from consistently authentic (although imperfect) Christians. This may be more difficult than we realize for those of us raised in unhealthy families.

There is a direct, three-step path from our families of childhood to our churches of adulthood: (1) We get our concepts of God primarily from our relationships with our parents. (2) If we were raised in unhealthy families by abusive or neglectful parents, we are likely to see God as harsh and demanding or perhaps as distant and disinterested. (3) As adults, we tend to choose churches that proclaim the kind of God we "met" in our families as children. Therefore, those of us who grew up in unhealthy, shame-based families will gravitate toward unhealthy, shame-based churches. Appendix B contrasts some common traits of shame-full and grace-full church families. Use it to help you assess your current church's spiritual health.

As your child grows, tailor your teaching to fit his or her level of understanding. Learning something about child development will help immensely here; praying for wisdom helps even more. (See Jas 1:5 for encouragement.) Eventually, you can connect Jesus to God the Father. One creative mother began this process by explaining, "Jesus is God looking like a very kind man so we won't be scared of him." This mom figured that was reasonably accurate theology for a three-year-old.

Whatever our children's ages, we must remember that our "walk" always teaches more powerfully than our "talk." We may go to church with our children three or four times a week and have family worship twice a day. And yet the prevailing patterns of our daily life and interactions with our children will more deeply influence their spiritual development than any of our formal religious routines. However, this doesn't mean that either we or our faith have to be perfect to be effective.

I am encouraged by the father who asked Jesus to heal his son while honestly acknowledging that his own faith in Jesus was mixed with unbelief. Jesus worked powerfully in this man's son despite the father's imperfect faith. (See Mk 9:17-27 for the whole story.) Obviously, both the father and his faith were flawed. Thankfully, God blesses us and our children because of his gracious love, not because of our good lives.

But what if our lives have been anything but good? What if we have profoundly misrepresented God through our neglect, rage . . . or even abuse? Or maybe we have lived "look-good lives" in our churches and communities but have been selfish, sulking pagans within our homes. Our older children may know us as faithless or phony—or both.

Teaching Older Children: Right Now

Even when we did not do it right *from the start,* we can start doing it right *now.* Each of our situations is different, but here are some general guidelines to get started.

1. Start by getting right with God. Ask God to forgive you for

spiritually abusing your children and for any other wrongs you have not confessed. Thank him for his forgiveness and gracious love. Finally, ask God the Spirit to guide and empower you as you seek to change, and ask him to prepare your children's hearts for change too.

2. Begin immediately to acknowledge to your children that you have misrepresented God. Confess to them as many specific incidents as you can remember, and explain how your behavior misrepresented God. For instance, if you have been an agnostic, confess that you have taught that God is either nonexistent or unimportant. If you have been excessively demanding and perfectionistic, explain to your children that the God of Scripture is not like that. *Continue to confess* as you identify ways you have spiritually abused your children.

3. Ask your children to forgive you. But do not assume they will, especially if you have not modeled forgiveness. Be prepared for their anger, their contempt, their disinterest, or a dozen other responses beside forgiveness.

4. Tell your children that you are practicing new choices so you can change the ways you relate to God and to them. Explain that you will continue to change your "talk" and your "walk" as you learn more truth about God and how he wants you to live.

5. If they will listen, talk to your children about what you are learning. Invite them to go with you, if you have found a healthier church family than the one in which they were raised.

6. "Walk" (that is, model) what you are learning; don't just "talk" it. Remember, even when your children refuse to listen to you, they will get the message loud and clear as you begin to change your behavior. For example, consider giving your child a gift for no reason except to express your love. That's what God does. You might want to include a note asking your child to forgive you for teaching the lie of "earned gift." Incidentally, this gift does not have to cost money. It could be a handwritten voucher for a pleasant activity or a helpful service which you are promising to do with or for your child.

You will probably think of a dozen more ways you can live out what you are learning about God. And as you practice these new choices, your children will be watching, listening and learning too.

Other family members will also be watching and listening. And some of them may not approve of your new choices.

Facing Family Disapproval

As we study Scripture to see Jesus more clearly and learn about God, we may discover that we feel *more* loved by our heavenly Parent but *less* by our earthly ones. If your parents are deeply entrenched in a joyless, graceless system of rigid rule-keeping that they have mistaken for biblical Christianity, they may question your salvation as well as your sanity when you begin to change. Or your unchurched parents and family may ridicule you and your faith. Whether you're called a rebellious fool or a religious fanatic, you will probably feel rejected and isolated from your family.

To further complicate the matter, the more insecure our parents are, the more they will perceive our new choices as personal attacks. They usually try to get us "back in line" by withdrawing their affection and approval. This takes as many forms as there are families.

In extreme cases, our parents and/or families may sever contact with us. If that happens, we will need the loving comfort of our heavenly Father and the support and encouragement of our church family more than ever.

And remember, as we learn to depend upon God in our painful experiences, we are teaching our children to trust him in the painful experiences that await them.

Personal Reflection

Here are some of the ways the Bible describes God. After you read through this partial list of God's attributes, study and meditate upon each one.

Attributes of God

1. *God is compassionate* as demonstrated in his mercy and lovingkindness. Psalm 103:8: "The LORD is compassionate and gracious, slow to anger, abounding in love."

2. *God is forgiving* because of his grace and mercy. Jesus paid our sin debts so that God could forgive sin while remaining holy and just. Ephesians 1:7: "In [Christ] we have redemption through his blood, the forgiveness of sins, in accordance with the riches of God's grace." (See also Rom 3:23-26.)

3. *God is holy* because of his absolute moral excellence. Luke 1:49: "For the Mighty One has done great things for me—holy is his name."

4. *God is immutable:* he never changes. Hebrews 13:8: "Jesus Christ is the same yesterday and today and forever."

5. *God is just* because he always acts fairly, in accordance with his nature. Deuteronomy 32:4: "He is the Rock, his works are perfect, and all his ways are just. A faithful God who does no wrong, upright and just is he."

6. *God is loving* because it is his nature and not because of anything we do to elicit his love. His love is expressed in actions toward us. 1 John 4:16: "God is love."

7. *God is omnipotent:* he has unlimited power and ability. Jeremiah 32:17: "You have made the heavens and the earth by your great power and outstretched arm. Nothing is too hard for you."

8. *God is omnipresent:* he is present everywhere in the universe at the same time. God is never "absent." Jeremiah 23:23-24: " 'Am I only a God nearby,' declares the LORD, 'and not a God far away? Can anyone hide in secret places so that I cannot see him?' declares the LORD. 'Do not I fill heaven and earth?' declares the LORD."

9. *God is omniscient:* he has unlimited knowledge and wisdom. Psalm 139:2-4: "You know when I sit and when I rise; you perceive my thoughts from afar. You discern my going out and my lying down; you are familiar with all my ways. Before a word is on my tongue you know it completely, O LORD."

10. *God is righteous* because he does only what is right and is free from any wrongdoing. Psalm 145:17: "The LORD is righteous in all his ways and loving toward all he has made."

11. *God is sovereign* because he rules supremely over all creation. Daniel 4:35: "He does as he pleases with the powers of heaven and the peoples of the earth. No one can hold back his hand or say to him: 'What have you done?' "

12. *God is truthful* because, in accordance with his nature, he cannot lie. Titus 1:1-2: ". . . for the faith of God's elect and the knowledge of the truth that leads to godliness—a faith and knowledge resting on the hope of eternal life, which God, who does not lie, promised before the beginning of time."

As you reflect on each attribute, ask yourself these two questions.

1. How would my daily life change if I made practical choices based upon the reality of this kind of God? (For example, if God is really forgiving, and if I have asked for forgiveness, then I can stop punishing myself for past sins.)

2. What are some practical ways I can teach my child/children about these attributes of God? (For example, since God is truthful, I must consistently be scrupulously truthful or I will misrepresent God. When my children see me "paying a price" for being truthful—returning excess change at the market, for example—I will talk about our truthful God wanting us to be truthful too.)

Looking Ahead

In this chapter we have learned that we'll see God more accurately when we look into the Scriptures and turn away from those who have misrepresented him. In the next chapter, we'll discover that a remarkably similar refocusing is required if we want to see ourselves and our children accurately.

7
We Can Learn to Really Love Our Children

*M*argery *Williams's beloved story* The Velveteen Rabbit *tells about* childhood relationships, talking toys—and much, much more.

"What is REAL? asked the Rabbit.... "Does it mean having things that buzz inside you and a stick-out handle?"

"Real isn't how you are made," said the Skin Horse. "It is a thing that happens to you. When a child loves you for a long, long time, not just to play with, but REALLY loves you, then you become Real."[1]

We can all identify with the Rabbit's quest to be special and "real" by feeling valued and loved. And we suspect that the wise old Horse is right: our concepts of ourselves as lovable and valuable develop within loving relationships in our homes.

Overwhelming research evidence demonstrates that *children* who have healthy self-concepts usually have *parents* with healthy self-concepts.[2] Therefore, evaluating and correcting our own self-concepts is one of the most important steps on our journey to increasingly shame-free parenting.

Just as the Rabbit needed a child's love, children need their parents' love to make them feel special and real. Children need to be valued for just *being themselves.* This sense of who and what we really are is our self-concept. (I will use the terms self-image and self-concept interchangeably, since both refer to the way in which we see ourselves.)

Does this mean that in order to develop sound self-images, all we need is parents who love us? Unfortunately, the answer is no. "Self-images" are actually "mirror-images," and even loving parents can be very marred "mirrors."

"Mirror, Mirror, on the wall, who's the fairest of them all?" The evil queen in "Snow White" was sure she would always hear the truth when she asked that question of her magical talking mirror. As children, we assumed that our "mirrors" also told the truth—that what we saw mirrored in our parents' faces as they took care of us was an accurate reflection of our true identity and worth.

We could not understand that, in reality, what we saw in our parents' faces, heard in their voices and received from their hands reflected who *they* were, not who *we* were. And we had no way of knowing that even *loving* parents can become horribly marred mirrors when they are impaired by their own poor self-concepts and bound by shame that prevents them from recognizing and resolving their life-dominating problems.

Behavior-Based Identity

How do impaired parents in shame-based families transmit, usually unintentionally, false messages about their children's identities and worth? What do these messages sound and look like? And how can we tell whether we received any of them? The following poem provides one answer to these crucial questions.

He'll Never Drop a Pea Again

As a child, he scooped peas
onto his fork.
One day a pea dropped
onto the table.
That's the day he learned
from his father
that he was clumsy,
would amount to
nothing,
a lecture that stretched
over the years until
nothing
was left of the boy
who scooped peas.
Now he spears them
one-by-one.[3]

Dropping peas, spilling milk, tracking mud and scores of other normal childhood behaviors are regarded in healthy families simply as behaviors that can be remedied with other behaviors. But in shame-based families, with their external focus and unrealistic expectations of perfection, these behaviors assume incredible power.

A child's behavior can become a definitive statement about that child's identity and worth. Instead of hearing, "One of your peas escaped onto the table," a child receives parental prophecies of unredeemable wretchedness and future failure.

Figure 7-1 contrasts two styles of parental response to childhood behaviors. Which statements sound more familiar as you recall your childhood? Which are heard more frequently in your home today?

Behavior as Behavior	**Behavior as Identity**

With First-Grade Child

| 1. "Oh dear, there goes the milk. Paper towels will soak that up in a jiffy." | 1. "Oh great, now look what you did. You are always so clumsy and careless." |
| MESSAGE: Paper towels are good for cleaning up spilled liquids. | MESSAGE: I am a clumsy and careless person. |

With Fifth-Grade Child

| 2. "I need you to clean up your model-building materials so I can set the dinner table." | 2. "You are such a selfish slob. Just look at all this junk you left in the dining room again." |
| MESSAGE: I am expected to clean up after myself. | MESSAGE: I am a selfish slob-person. My interests and things are junk. |

With Senior-High Child

| 3. "I'm not sure I understand exactly what you're saying, let alone if I agree with you. But I can tell this is important to you, so run it by me again." | 3. "Can't you ever say anything that makes sense? Where in the world did you get such a stupid idea, anyway? Certainly not from anyone in *our* family. I don't want to hear anymore of your harebrained opinions in this house, Mr Know-it-all." |
| MESSAGE: My ideas are important and respected even when they differ from those of my folks. I am learning to think for myself. | MESSAGE: My ideas don't make sense and I am stupid. My ideas are unimportant, unwelcomed and bad when they differ from those of my folks. |

Figure 7-1.

Which statements sound more familiar? One Christian mother I know gasped in stunned surprise when she first heard about the "behavior as behavior" messages.

She explained, "I had no idea parents ever talked to their kids like that—I mean as if they were *real people*. It just never entered my mind! I never remember hearing anything but 'you're so this and you're so that,' you know—so stupid, so selfish." Tears began to spill down her face as she added in a whisper, "So it never occurred to me to do anything different with my kids."

Of course it didn't. How could it? Like most of us, she naturally assumed her parents related to her the way *all* parents are supposed to relate to *all* children. So like the dutiful daughter she is, she simply passed along the self-concept-bashing that had been passed to her.

The messages received from the two kinds of parental responses in figure 7-1 are astoundingly different, aren't they? In effect, the children were learning expectations related to their identities. And since children naturally, self-protectively seek to please, those who are labeled "stupid," "clumsy" and so on soon learn to live *down* to their parents' expectations.

Why do unwise parents magnify a child's natural childhood behaviors until they obscure the child's intrinsic God-given worth? As we've already mentioned, children's behavior-based identity is often rooted in their parents' need to have perfect children. So a C on a report card can equal an identity of "you're a lazy and stupid person and an embarrassment to our family."

Remember too that parents' *nonverbal* interactions with their children convey identity messages even more powerfully than words. For instance, if a father says "I love you" but regularly batters his son or rapes his daughter, his behaviors muffle his words. His children do not receive the message, "I am a lovable person." They hear instead, "I am a person who gets hurt and humiliated by people who love me."

There is a world of difference between an identity label that reads *Lovable* and one that says *Deserves Pain to Get Love*. And as we have already observed, since children assume their parents know and tell the truth about their genuine worth, the children begin to see themselves accordingly. Therefore the *Lovable*-labeled child's world of personal, spiritual and relational expectations will bear about as much resemblance to that of the child wearing the *Deserves Pain* label as earth does to Mars. (Perhaps this explains, in part, why some of us often feel like extraterrestrials when we are with adults from healthy families!)

Labels from Loving Parents

Parents' actions override their words in less dramatically destructive ways too. Consider Warren's case.

Warren is a successful young professional who serves in several leadership positions in his church. He was raised by Christian parents who frequently articulated their love for him. But something happened in the transmission from their lips to his ears. Here is how Warren, a workaholic in the business world, described it to his Christian counselor.

"I feel like such a jerk," Warren said in a bewildered tone. "Why should I be killing myself and sacrificing my family by trying so hard to be important at the office and at church? I mean, I didn't come from one of those 'dysfunctional families' everybody is talking about. I can remember my folks telling me that they loved me."

Warren's eyes and voice dropped as he continued, "But somehow I had a hard time believing them. Dad was always so busy with his law practice, you know. I use to beg him to come to my soccer and basketball games when I was a kid. He'd always promise to be there, tell me how proud of me he was, then never show up. Eventually, I just stopped asking and hoping. And my mom stayed really busy too—at church, volunteering in the hospital and later working part-time. I feel selfish and really guilty about this, but I guess I always thought that if people loved you they would want to spend time with you."

Is Warren guilty of being selfish? I don't think so. Were his parents heartless brutes? Certainly not; they loved Warren. However, his parents broadcasted a lot of nonverbal "static" that interfered with clear transmission of their verbal love message. And their son grew up wearing a label that read, *I am so unimportant that I have to work harder than other people to be noticed and loved.*

No wonder Warren is exhausted most of the time. And no wonder he doesn't take the time to show his children *by his actions* that he values and loves them. He has been far too busy working hard in order to be noticed and to earn love.

During counseling, Warren realized that his father's treatment of him carbon-copied the treatment Warren's father had received from *his* father—Warren's grandfather.

"I can't believe what all of us 'good, Christian fathers' have done in our family—including me," Warren exclaimed. "My granddad was a great guy. I mean he truly loved the Lord—my dad did too. They never knew that their neglect hurt their sons so much."

There are other identity-distorting labels hand-woven in loving Christian homes. In fact, sometimes we very loving Christian parents can cripple our kids with *kindness* in our sincere efforts to give them the comfort and attention we never received from our parents. Unwittingly we're weaving labels for our children that read, *I am incompetent and helpless.*

Others of us want to shield our children from contact with the dark and dangerous side of life we were exposed to by inattentive and/or impaired parents. Trying to hermetically seal our children within perfectly safe personal environments unintentionally transmits more than our fear-tinged love. Our children will likely perceive our concerns as evidence that they are too fragile to survive out in the real world. They also receive the blatantly unbiblical message that *God* cannot be trusted to care for them, since *we* seem to have to do it. This is particularly harmful and ironic considering that only God can help us achieve the truly healthy and balanced self-concepts we want to gain for ourselves and give to our children.

Correcting Self-Concepts

Although some people are far less sin-marred than others, none are perfect. Therefore, we will never see ourselves accurately if we insist upon looking to other human beings for a sense of identity and worth. To see ourselves clearly, we need a perfect mirror. It is likely that each of us possesses it already—perhaps within arm's reach.

Who could be better than our original Designer when it comes to showing us an honest and accurate view of ourselves? In James 1:23-25, God describes the Bible's mirroring function for those who sincerely desire to know themselves. And God promises he will bless us when we continue living out what we learn from his Word rather than casually consulting it and then forgetting its truths.

Curiously, many Christians who diligently read God's Word seem blind to passages that establish our identity in Christ. Christian churches and leaders traditionally have taught that we are unworthy of God's gift of grace. They're right. That's why grace is a gift—we couldn't be worthy/good enough to earn it. However, in an apparently sincere effort to emphasize grace, some of these churches and leaders also teach that we are worthless. Nothing could be further from the truth.

Unworthy or Worthless?
The price paid for an object establishes its value. In fact, *every buyer subjectively attributes worth to his or her purchases.* And the purchase price reveals the buyer's personal opinion regarding the value of that purchase. For example, an avocado has no objective value in and of itself. I usually pass them by—especially if they are bruised and still overpriced. Yet if I want to make guacamole, I subjectively bestow sufficient value upon a ripe (and usually bruised) avocado to warrant paying its purchase price.

I'll admit my analogy springs from a supermarket's produce department rather than a seminary's theology department. And obviously it falls far short of explaining the mystery of our worth to God. Nevertheless, there is a common theme. For some incomprehensibly gracious reason, and despite the fact that we are all hopelessly bruised by sin, God chooses to make of us something infinitely more wonderful than guacamole. He makes us his adopted heirs and kingdom priests.

And what is the purchase price God paid to accomplish his goal? "The precious blood of Christ," 1 Peter 1:18 declares. Yes! I know it sounds impossibly grandiose to say it, but by the price he paid, God has openly established our worth. For when it came to our purchase price, God was more concerned about what he "saved" than what he spent.

Are we unworthy? Absolutely. Are we worthless? Absolutely not! This baffling blend of truths is an unfathomable paradox to us, but I don't think it bothers God at all. What's more, it suggests other paradoxical aspects of human personhood, such as great potential and firm limitations or the capacity for both unblinking cruelty and self-less compassion.

God sees us perfectly and describes us precisely in Scripture. So, learning to see ourselves as God sees us requires looking into our perfect mirror, the Bible. Changing our self-concepts does not usually happen quickly or easily. We need to be persistent. We cannot expect to totally alter twenty, thirty or more years of thinking about our-selves in a month—or a year.

As we continue to replace distorted messages with God's truth, we will increasingly relate to ourselves, our children and others with appropriate love. For example, as we choose to change "I am so stu-pid" to "I made a mistake" messages to ourselves, we will begin to change our messages to our children. And as we consistently (but not perfectly) practice these new choices, we will help our children learn to see themselves as God sees them—and thereby change their self-deprecating, unbiblical self-labeling.

If we really get serious about this business of correcting our un-healthy and unbiblical self-concepts so that we can help our children do the same, we will likely come face to face with the "cookie-cutter syndrome." When we do, we may discover that our childhood fam-ilies lacked an extremely significant element: sincere respect for the unique expression of God's image in each individual.

Clones or Kids?

"You've got to be kidding, right?" That's how Marla responded to the idea that consistently adequate parents don't expect everyone in the family to have the same personality, abilities and interests. Quiet, shy Marla still felt the sting from her professionally-oriented parents' sharp rejection when she chose to attend a local secretarial school instead of a distinguished four-year college as her brothers and sister had.

Marla's parents seemed to want identical clones rather than individual kids. This is true in many unhealthy families where parents and children seem stamped out of the same mold, like gingerbread men from a cookie cutter. It takes time and mental energy for parents to observe newborns so they can begin to understand each infant's unique temperament. Parents' time and mental energy are usually unavailable luxuries in hurting families.

I am not advocating we jump through hoops for our children. But when they are very young we must be flexible enough to do most of the "bending"—adjusting our own "styles" to those of our children. (I use "style" to describe each person's *unique way* of interacting with his or her environment based on inborn temperament plus physical and intellectual characteristics.) As our children grow, we can appropriately expect them to flex more and do their share of appropriately fitting in without requiring them to abandon their individuality.

All of this can be a formidable challenge for those of us raised with the cookie-cutter mentality. First, we may not have a clue about how to recognize our God-given, individual "styles," let alone how to use and enjoy them. Second, we may struggle to reconcile our genuine love for our children with the deep resentment we feel when trying to give them what we may never have received: *permission to be fully the unique individual God created.*

In addition, as appalling as it is to face, some of us are squeezing our children into the very molds our parents fashioned for us. In effect, we use our children as keys to unlock the storehouse of parental approval which has been partly or completely refused us thus far. That's what I did with Becky.

"Loyalty" vs. Individuality

Good mothers have daughters who play the piano. I grew up believing that was an immutable law of the universe, like gravity. I knew that my mother was pleased with me and felt better about herself when she perceived that she had raised a daughter who was a "good" mother. So I set out to please my mother by squeezing my daughter into a musical mold.

Becky has a lovely alto voice and a great deal of musical ability. When she was eight, she actually performed two of her own short piano compositions at recitals in her teacher's home. Becky is also very athletic. In fact, Becky has a wide variety of interests and abilities and she was not thrilled by the prospect of putting all her eggs in a Steinway basket. That created a real crisis for me—*again.*

You'd think I would have outgrown my parent-pleasing crises by then. (I had been married thirteen years; Dave was eleven and Becky was nearly nine.) In truth, I didn't see that it *was* a "parent-pleasing crisis." All I knew was that I had this relentless compulsion to force Becky to love the piano. No doubt you've already guessed correctly that the more I did that, the more she hated it.

I was weakening my relationship with my daughter by making her feel *less* accepted so that I could strengthen my relationship with my mother and make myself feel *more* accepted. But I saw none of this then. In fact, to feel the power of the intergenerational assault upon individuality in some families, you need to understand that *I sincerely believed I was doing what a good mother should do!*

I'm not exactly sure what happened. Maybe I finally heard Becky when she said, for the zillionth time, "Just because you loved to play the piano doesn't mean I have to. I'm not you!" (She understood more about individuality at eight than I did at thirty-three.) After Becky left for school that morning, I prayed and wept before the Lord about the entire situation.

God reminded me of all the times my mother had conveyed that my piano recitals, radio program and other musical activities were more about *her* being a good mother than they were about my using my God-given ability. I saw too that I had believed Becky's musical performance was a commentary about *me* and my parenting abilities rather than a commentary about *her* and her musical abilities. As long as I held this children-exist-to-validate-their-parents perspective, I *had* to make Becky keep taking piano lessons so that the world would know I was a good mother!

It sounds melodramatic as I write this now, but that morning I took a momentous step in my life and my parenting. Perhaps for the first time, I clearly understood the need to *transfer my primary loyalty from being my parent's child to being my child's parent.* Face on tear-soaked carpet, I felt my heart would break with regret and remorse. Before God I vowed to reorder my skewed priorities and begin appreciating and honoring Becky for the precious, unique person she is.

After school I told Becky she could stop piano lessons at the end of the month if she was certain about her choice. I semi-seriously added that when she was an adult I was not going to feel guilty if she said her folks should have made her continue taking piano lessons. Becky was relieved and grateful, and she promised I'd never hear that. And I never have, although we've laughed a lot about it.

Again we confront the truth that we must learn to be *healthier persons* when we want to be *healthier parents.* Specifically, we will not be able to teach our children to honor individuality in themselves and others if we ourselves have never learned this lesson.

The "Weight" of Individuality

Perhaps some would question my use of "honor" with regard to individuality. It may sound a little grandiose. Why not "value," or even "esteem"? You will recall from chapter one that the original Hebrew meaning of "honor" is "heavy," and that evolved into the concept of *weighty importance* or *great influence.*

Clearly recognizing and openly acknowledging the heavy influence of each person's God-designed uniqueness is at the heart of honoring each person's individuality. This has clear implications for parents. God thinks children's individuality is of such heavy importance that he tells parents to customize their child-rearing to fit each child's unique characteristics. Scripture calls this unique personal style "his [or her] way" in Proverbs 22:6.[4]

In healthy families, respect and honor between generations flow in both directions. Therefore, as our children mature, we need to help them learn to appreciate and honor *our* individuality too. Additionally, there is an intergenerational flow of honoring or dishonoring individuality between our *parents* and our *children.*

If our parents are significantly shame-bound and insecure, they will not respect differences easily. They will tend to perceive *different* choices as criticism of *their* choices. So some of their grandchildren's choices may be very threatening!

For instance, Tommy was more skilled with a French horn than a football. He learned quickly and painfully that his paternal grandparents saw him as a misfit. "Every generation of men in our family has won athletic scholarships!" said Grandpa. "What is blowing a horn gonna get you? You ought to be out on the football field." Grandma too communicated her disappointment with Tommy. She told him how proud she was of his cousin who had made the varsity squad. She wouldn't even attend Tommy's recital.

Robert, Tommy's father, finally confronted his parents about their insensitive and dishonoring behavior. They said he wasn't making any sense, and besides, didn't he know how important sports were in a young kid's life? When his parents consistently refused to change, Robert and his wife chose to visit less often rather than continue exposing Tommy to his grandparents' assaults on his individuality.

Certainly, it may take more effort to get to know and appreciate children who are distinctly different from us. But we and our children will be richly rewarded when we do. We will all learn a lot about ourselves and each other. And in the process, we will understand more about God's plan for the church to be a family where every member is important. Remember that the goal for our families is for *each* member to feel highly valued and deeply loved for himself or herself.

Personal Reflection

The following Bible verses will help you begin seeing yourself as God sees you.

☐ John 1:12; 1 Peter 2:9 (I am a child of God and I belong to him.)
☐ Romans 8:35-39 (I am loved by God and nothing can separate me from his love.)
☐ Ephesians 1:4 (I am chosen by God.)
☐ Ephesians 2:18; 3:12 (I have access to God through Jesus.)
☐ Colossians 2:13-14 (I am forgiven and my sin-debt is paid.)
☐ Romans 8:1 (I am not condemned.)
☐ Philippians 4:13 (I am strengthened for all tasks to which God calls me.)
☐ 1 Corinthians 6:19; John 14:16 (My body is the Holy Spirit's abode.)
☐ Romans 5:1 (I have peace with God through my Lord Jesus Christ.)
☐ Colossians 1:13 (I have been rescued from the dominion of darkness and brought into the kingdom of God's Son.)

Using your journal or a special notebook, write each verse, a personalized summary, and a past, present or future application. Each page of your journal or notebook could be headed with a statement like: *These verses tell me what my heavenly Father really thinks about me. Lord, help me believe your message about my identity.*

Here's an example of how one entry might look.

Colossians 2:13-14

> I am forgiven of all my sins because Jesus paid the purchase price for me. I don't need to continue to punish myself for the abortion I had when I got pregnant in high school. God knows my heart, so he knows I have sincerely repented. That sin does not make me ineligible for God's gracious blessings.

Begin memorizing the verses that are most meaningful to you. Perhaps you can get together with other Christian friends to study and discuss these verses and others that tell you how God sees you.

In your Christian bookstore you'll find Bible study guides available on this topic. I like *Self-Esteem: Seeing Ourselves As God Sees Us* by Jack Kuhatschek (IVP).

If your children are young, pray for wisdom about how to give verbal and nonverbal messages that tell them how unique and special they are.

If your children are older, tell them what you're learning about God's view of us.

Confess to your children and seek forgiveness for conveying wrong messages about their worth and dishonoring their individuality. Give specific examples. Our failures to honor individuality are not always as blatant as saying to a child, "Why can't you be like your sister?" We do it in a subtle way, for instance, when we always refer to our sons as "the boys"—as if they were sort of a male conglomerate. Or when we refuse to let our children dress and decorate their rooms according to their individual tastes (within reasonable but not rigid limits).

Looking Ahead

As we've seen, childhood identity messages establish our expectations for ourselves and for others. Like knights to Jerusalem, children from shame-bound families march off to adulthood on a crusade for the holy grail of perfection. And with about as much success.

8
We Can Learn to Have Realistic Expectations

*M*ost of my parenting was done in a Disneyland zip code.

With all the unrealistic expectations I cherished for myself and my children, I was a lot more at home in "Fantasyland" than in "Reality City." Most of these expectations betrayed my perfectionistic performing and pleasing approach to life.

I once heard perfectionists defined as those people who take great pains in life—and give them to others. Ouch! As a recovering perfectionist I'm sure that two of my "others" were my children. I'm also convinced there is a better and more biblical way to live and to parent.

Since many of us were taught that parents must push for perfection or their kids will stop trying and fail completely, we may get pretty anxious at the prospect of surrendering our motivational arsenal of shaming "not-good-enoughs." In the following pages, we'll discover several healthier, non-shaming alternatives for encouraging our children to be all God created them to be. But first, let's examine some of our expectations for ourselves and our children.

Expectations About Ourselves

True or false: Mistakes are as much a part of parenting as kids are. Our answers to this one-question quiz betray our most basic beliefs about ourselves and our children.

I realize I am sounding a familiar refrain here. However, from observing my own and others' lives, I've discovered that we need to hear repeatedly the truth that *human beings are, among other things, mistake-makers.*

The ancient "I-can-be-perfect-like-God" lie (as old as Eve and the serpent) is subtly seductive and incredibly resilient. Even when regularly buffeted by the biblical truth of human fallenness and the unavoidable signs of our own fallibility, this lie "takes a licking but keeps on ticking!" So, we aren't surprised to hear it ticking in the heartbeat of our parenting goals.

1. I can be a perfect parent. Most of us are "wanna-be" parents. We "wanna-be" perfect. Now, few if any of us would declare that we *are,* or ever *have been,* perfect parents. It's just that we want to be, and many of us believe down deep that if only we read the right books, attend the right seminars, find the right church and really, *really* try hard, we *can* be perfect parents.

A few years ago I would have been surprised and offended to hear my parenting expectations described as perfectionistic. After all, I simply wanted to

☐ know the correct answer to every possible parenting question;

☐ remain absolutely calm and in control in every possible parenting crisis; and

☐ be totally free from fear, anger or fatigue under every possible parenting pressure.

In short, I wanted to be a combination of June Cleaver, Mother Teresa, Dr. Joyce Brothers and Betty Crocker! What's unrealistic about that?

I can chuckle about such perfectionistic expectations now, but for many of us they were (or still are) serious aspirations—deadly serious. When we target parenting *perfection* as our only appropriate goal, we slay all hope for parenting *satisfaction* and we condemn ourselves to a life sentence of regret.

We inevitably end up feeling like parenting failures when we begin by demanding parenting perfection. Curiously (unless we recognize the familiar all-or-nothing thinking typical of shame-full families), the second expectation extreme commences where the first concludes.

2. I will be a total failure as a parent. In that earliest and most influential educational institution we call "family," we may have learned that children's needs are insatiable and impossible to meet. Therefore, we may take a fatalistic approach to parenting: even when we do our job, we don't expect to enjoy the results!

Many of us had overwhelmed, poorly functioning parents who did not acknowledge and address their own life-dominating problems. Instead of admitting that they were impaired in their capacities to adequately meet our legitimate childhood needs and desires, they told us we were selfish and demanding. Based on our parent-shaped understanding, we logically concluded that the problem was our "insatiable" needs, not our parents' limitations.

Of course all children *are* selfish and demanding at times. But in many dysfunctional families, children think "selfish" is a middle name. That was Bonnie's experience with a workaholic father and a self-absorbed mother.

"In third grade I really wanted to join Campfire Girls like my friends," Bonnie explained. "When I asked her, my mom said, 'I've got more to do than run all over town buying uniforms and driving you to some stupid meetings.' Being a kid, you know, I cried and begged her to let me join. She told me I was being a selfish brat and thought only about myself."

Bonnie continued, "That's just one example of how it always was until I eventually learned to stop wanting anything that required help from my folks. Later, I panicked when my own kids asked me to get involved in some of the things they wanted to do at church. Then, as I tried it, I was shocked because I really didn't have to do *that* much for them to enjoy themselves in some super activities." She concluded by observing, "It isn't easy to do what's right for kids and let them enjoy themselves too, but it's not impossible either."

Bonnie expected to be a total failure as a parent because she grew up believing that children's needs and desires are simply too overwhelming for *any* parent to handle. We can see that Bonnie's expectations of herself as a parent were closely tied to her expectations of her children. This is true of all parents.

Expectations About Our Children

Have you ever wished that your *kids* had read Dr. Spock's baby books so *they* would know how they were expected to behave? As parents, *we* certainly know how they're expected to behave. But often our kids just don't fit the formula.

I suppose there are as many different expectations about children as there are different parents. Let's look at three of the unrealistic expectations that seem to be most troublesome for those of us who grew up in shame-based families.

1. My children are out to get me. Have you ever felt that your child was "out to get you"? That's the phrase Ben used to describe his perception of his five-year-old son, Matt.

Ben was working through a lot of pain from being raised in an alcoholic family. In that process, he began to realize that he tended to view nearly every situation in life as a commentary on his personal worth. And when Ben felt inadequate in any interaction, as he often did, he saw the other person involved as "out to get him" by making him look bad. That's what he thought Matt was doing when he misbehaved one night when Ben's boss came for dinner. What the boss probably saw as normal five-year-old mischief, Ben found abnormal and humiliating.

As Ben began to accept his identity in Christ and experience less shame, he became less self-focused in his relationships—including his parenting. And when Ben started reading about human development and child discipline, he was better prepared for Matt's behavioral ups and downs rather than taking them all so personally.

We all tend to take our children's behavior personally to some degree. The more we do, the more we will expect them to share our perceptions. But we can work on getting free from such overreactions.

2. *My children need to be as upset about their mistakes as I am.* I had stopped at McDonald's to have a cold drink during my drive to Indianapolis when I noticed the two people at the next table. I could hear every word spoken between the deeply troubled woman and her male companion.

He looked unconcerned, but her face reflected the enormity of the tragedy: he had received a poor report of some kind and had told her about it. Was it her father newly diagnosed with cancer? Or perhaps her husband losing his job? Actually, her calm companion appeared to be no more than seven or eight years old and he called her Mom.

This mom went on and on verbally painting a dark picture of prophetic doom. Clearly, she was determined to generate in that second- or third-grader the same perception of tragedy that was contorting her attractive face.

Didn't he realize that he'd never get into a good college if he didn't snap out of it? And hadn't he learned that just a college degree isn't really enough in today's economy? How did he expect to get into a top graduate school? And then Mom delivered the "zinger": didn't he want her and Dad to be proud of him? During all this, the boy sat expressionless, looking at his French fries. He never glanced at his mom's face.

Perhaps this mother grew up in a home where *making* a mistake is the same as *being* a mistake and where failing at *something* makes *you* a failure. Whatever the case, she seems to be teaching her son these shame-based "performance-equals-personhood" lies. The more we bought into this lie growing up, the more demands we will place on our children's performance in school, on the athletic field and everywhere else. In fact, by constantly scrutinizing and emphasizing performance, we may convey to our children that their successful performances are *all* we truly value about them. And not only do we tend to constantly watch our children's performances, we closely watch *others* watching them. Especially when our parents are the others.

Frogs or Princes?

This overemphasis on our children's visible behavior, in contrast to their inner being, foreshadows the third unrealistic expectation many shame-bound parents face.

3. *My children must be perfect so they can rescue me from the shame of imperfection.* When we expect to have perfect children, we are living in a fairy tale just as much as if we were frogs expecting our offspring to be princes or princesses! Yet we do it all the time. Here's how this fairy tale unfolds.[1]

Our parents (and theirs before them) hoped and longed for a perfect prince or princess to rescue them from the dreaded curse of their despised froggishness—obvious imperfection. Early we sensed their longings and made them our own. With our parents' expectant gazes fixed upon us, we tried to be perfect so we could make them feel better about themselves and be happy.

Alas, we failed miserably. So we waded through all the eligible frogs in our vicinity until we thought we found a prince, or princess, to marry. We hoped thereby to persuade the watching world (primarily our parents, of course) that *we* were actually princes or princesses after all. (The logic: a prince or princess would be too smart to marry a frog, so we couldn't really be frogs.) Imagine our horror at discovering, very soon after the wedding, that we imperfect frogs had actually married *other* imperfect frogs!

But all was not lost. We had another chance to prove that perfection oozed from our genetic pool. By producing perfect prince or princess children, we would be rescued from our froggishness and finally satisfy our watching parents once and for all. (The logic: everyone knows frogs could never give birth to princes or princesses; therefore, such perfect children must have perfect parents.)

At last we would prove that if frogs just try *hard* enough, they can become (or at least give birth to) princes and princesses. With so much riding on the perfect performance of our children—our personal worth, our parents' approval, even *their* personal worth—we must carefully, constantly scrutinize everything the children do for telltale signs of froggishness. Obviously, those disgusting hints of imperfection (mistakes, second-place finishes, less than all A's) must be dealt with swiftly and harshly. After all, a child's primary purpose in life is to make parents look good, isn't it? *We* certainly learned that lesson well. Our kids had better learn it too—the sooner the better.

Just harmless make-believe, right? I'm not so sure. Consider the "report card reflex" recently identified in major cities across the country. At report card time, school officials and child welfare professionals report an alarming increase in physical abuse of children whose report cards "upset their parents."[2] While the "report card reflex" is shocking, it is not surprising if, as I am suggesting, shame-bound parents see their children's performance primarily as a reflection of their own worth. These parents feel compelled to make their children take seriously the mission of making their parents look good—even if it kills them.

This "my-child-exists-to-validate-me" attitude may have been Wanda Holloway's prime motive when she was convicted of hiring a killer to murder the mother of her daughter's main cheerleading competitor. Apparently Mrs. Holloway hoped her daughter's competitor would be too distraught by her mother's death to continue participating in the junior-high cheerleading tryouts. Commenting on the value of "healthy competition," the school principal said, "After all, it is the American way. We all want our children to achieve. There is a part of Wanda Holloway in all of us."[3]

It is unlikely that any of us would so overidentify with our children's performances that we would kill to improve their chances of success. But, to our sorrow, many of us may detect "a part of Wanda Holloway" in our driven determination to make our children do not just *their* best but *the* best in all activities. (For their own good, of course.) We've been taught to call this *motivation.* I've begun to call it *emotional abuse:* praise of child-produced performance without affirmation of God-given worth.

While we can't be certain about Wanda Holloway's personal relationship with God, media reports said she was the organist at a church known for its emphasis on Bible study. This suggests that it is possible for us to listen regularly to the teaching of God's truth without letting it transform our minds and motives. And without new motives in our hearts, we will never use new motivation in our homes.

Encouraging Personal Growth in Ourselves and Our Children
The following suggestions aim for lifelong personal growth in ourselves and in our children with a biblical and balanced emphasis on inner being and outer doing.

1. Assess and alter your values. Figure 8-1 displays two contrasting motivational approaches reflecting different values. Use it to help you assess the values underlying your current motivational style.

What do you see here about your values regarding child motivation? Most of us probably will relate to something from both approaches. In Scripture we find Jesus rebuking religious leaders who emphasized outer behaviors to the neglect of inner being. We may be dismayed to discover that we've taken the same path for ourselves

Contrasting Self- and Child-Motivation Attitudes and Approaches

Internal Focus:
See Self/Child as Human Being

I belong to God by creation (and if I have asked Jesus to be my Savior and Lord, by salvation), so my major task is to know and love God and seek and do his will for my life.

My child belongs to God, so my major task is to help my child be the person God created by teaching him/her to know God.

I emphasize the internal perspective of developing my own and my child's characters.

I take a "long view" for the purpose of character development, e.g., letting my child learn the consequences of procrastinating by getting a poor grade on his/her science project done the night before it was due.

I talk *primarily* about my child as an authentically struggling Christian, a very thoughtful spouse, a tenderhearted boy or girl, a sincerely questioning teen, an honest employee, a wise parent, or a lover and student of Scripture.

I usually ask (myself and my child), "Did you enjoy yourself/learn anything?"

In myself and in my child, I affirm and reward "brave attempts" as well as obvious successes.

External Focus:
See Self/Child as Human "Doing"

I belong to my parents and to others who "need" and care for me. My major task is to please and perform for them (as perfectly as possible) so they will love/approve of me so that I can feel good about myself.

My child belongs to me, so I have the right to press my child into the service of my shame-based and perfectionistic needs.

I emphasize the external perspective of promoting and polishing my own and my child's performances.

I take a "short view" for the appearance of perfect performance, e.g., doing my child's science project myself the night before it is due so that my child maintains high grades.

I talk *primarily* about my child as the doctor, the ballet star, the select soccer hero, the youngest company vice president in history, the pee-wee league all-star, or the winner of the Sunday school's Scripture memorization contest.

I usually ask (myself and my child), "Did you win/were you the best?"

In myself and in my child, I affirm and reward winning only. ("Second place is no place!" If I don't do it perfectly, it is "garbage"!)

Figure 8-1.

and with our children. It is not easy to change long-standing values, but we can do it with God's help.

When our new, more biblical values begin to show up in new attitudes and behavior, parents and others may criticize our shift of emphasis from a person's performances to his or her inner qualities. It helps to find support and encouragement from other parents who share your new perspective.

2. *Compliment character qualities as well as performance.* At first this may feel awkward and strange, but it is an important element in developing a more biblical perspective. Our children need to hear us commenting to others on their inner qualities as much as or more than we recite their latest achievements in school, sports, business and so on. (Remember to take this same healthier perspective with yourself as well.)

Also remember to affirm and compliment your children warmly, frequently and *directly.* It is astounding how many adults from hurting families tell me they do not recall ever hearing either of their parents compliment them. Yet they learned as adults, often after a parent's death, that this parent praised them to adult friends or relatives.

In addition to affirming the child's helpfulness or honesty or patience, it is important to say occasionally, "I'm glad I have you for a daughter," or some other comment that indicates you like your child just for who he or she is, regardless or any particular traits he or she has.

3. *Redefine "success."* Without realizing it, for many years I defined success as *experiencing approval from the most significant person(s) in my life.* This approval-addicted attitude may ring a bell for you too.

Obviously we must redefine success for ourselves before we'll be able to teach our children its true meaning. We can begin with adopting appropriate goals, then working toward them by eliminating perfection and substituting authentic excellence. How motivated to stretch their skills can children be when they know from experience that they will always hear their parents say, "That's pretty good, but try harder" or "Yes, that's better, but you didn't . . ."?

If we learned to value nothing but perfection, that kind of comment will be about the most affirming we'll offer our children. Under our new definition of success, instead of first asking, "Did you win?" we could inquire about how our children felt about their levels of effort or enjoyment in competitive activities. We could begin to affirm and reward *brave attempts* even if they end in failure. This would require redefining failure as well as success.

4. *Redefine "failure."* "Failures are the pillars of success," says an ancient Hebrew proverb. That concept of failure seems positively absurd to adults raised in shame-based, perfection-worshiping families. These families operate by the unspoken motto *Second place is no place.* Mistakes become disasters and failures seem fatal.

In reality, mistakes, failures, errors and plain old "goofs" are normal parts of living. We must learn to believe this truth and teach it to our children. We must learn and teach also that failing doesn't make us failures. It simply proves we are exactly what the Bible says we are—imperfect humans.

Sometimes we worry that our children will become discouraged by mistakes and stop trying to achieve worthwhile goals. Actually, children tend to accept mistakes and move on without any negative impact on their next attempts when they know that they are loved and that they don't have to be perfect.

It won't be easy to relinquish our unrealistic and perfectionistic expectations, but we can do it. And we can also help our children unload this unbearable burden. Here's how Norma seized a "teachable moment" with her first-born, who had begun to be perfectionistic and constantly dissatisfied with herself. One school night, the fourth-grader was bemoaning some erasure marks on a math chart. Norma told her, "Mommy makes mistakes, and erasers were made because everyone else does too."

When Norma reported this dialog to her Christ-centered support group, she told us her daughter was amazed and relieved because she had thought grown-ups didn't made mistakes anymore! After the groans and laughter subsided, the group agreed that we had *all* believed that as children too, and we wished we had had a mom like Norma.

We cannot all *have* parents like Norma, but we can all *become* parents like Norma. You see, she grew up in an extremely chaotic alcoholic family. That's why Norma participates in her recovery group. When she became a Christian a few years ago, Norma asked God to help her become the mom her girls needed. God is doing that for Norma, and he'll do it for us.

Personal Reflection

Review figure 8-1.
□ Which child motivational attitudes sound more like yours?
□ What do you need to do to change your motivational style to one that more accurately reflects the reality of human imperfection?
□ How will you make the changes? Who or what could help you?
□ When will you begin?

Looking Ahead

Maybe you are well aware of your imperfection as a parent by now. Hang in there as we continue our trek to increasingly shame-free parenting! We're headed for learning about one of our most important yet problematic responsibilities: communicating with our children.

9
We Can Learn
to Communicate with
Talk and Touch

W*e're just not communicating!"*

As a therapist, I've heard that statement a lot of times. I've also said it in moments of frustration. How about you? Actually, we cannot "not communicate." If I fall silent during a strained conversation with a friend, I have not ceased communicating. I've simply switched from primarily verbal to solely nonverbal communication. I am saying silently, "I no longer want to talk about this with you."

We are always communicating *something.* In fact, it could be argued that if we don't affirm our children frequently, they may "hear" us saying that they are incompetent and unimportant. The vast majority of parents never intend to communicate messages like that—we just don't understand basic communication principles.

We may have thought that all we inherited from our families was

Grandma's silver or Dad's toolbox. A closer look may uncover an additional legacy of shame-bound family "rules" for talking and touching. This chapter is about recognizing and changing that hurtful heritage.

Remember that, in addition to words, communication includes nonverbal interactions like facial expression and touch. Many of us from unhealthy, shame-based families learned that talking and touching can be awkward and uncomfortable—even unsafe. It is not surprising that we might encounter special challenges when we seek to improve verbal and nonverbal communication with our children. Let's begin examining these challenges by tuning in to our talk.

Communicating with Talk

We've already seen some specific ways shame-based families can wound children with words by labeling them "stupid" or "clumsy" and by comparing them unfavorably with others. Now we broaden our focus to more general effects of the dysfunctional family's "Be Quiet" rule, and we'll contrast these effects with communication patterns in substantially shame-free families. As you consider these contrasting patterns, ask yourself which you learned as a child and which you are living and teaching in your family today.

Parental Listening vs. Not Listening

It may seem strange to begin our overview of verbal communication contrasts with *listening* instead of *talking.* But remember, this is aimed at *parents.* And as painful as it may be to admit, some of us fail to really listen to our children. Sometimes this includes me, I regret to say.

When Dave was in high school, he once asked me to stop mixing cookie dough and listen to him. I said that I *had* been listening, to which he replied, "I don't feel like you hear me when you won't stop and look at me."

Zap! I felt as if I'd taken a bullet in the heart. I suddenly realized that I'd been doing that to Dave and Becky for years. Sure, I had read about how parents could improve communication with children; I knew the importance of eye contact to make the other person feel "heard." What I did *not* know was how much my childhood learning short-circuited good communication principles.

I grew up believing that doing only one thing at a time was inexcusably inefficient. I specialized in multiplying my daily allotment of moments by cramming most of them with at least two activities. I was feeling smugly satisfied with myself, actually, on the afternoon of Dave's request: I was baking cookies and listening to him at the same time. But that afternoon, Dave needed a "laying on of ears and eyes" more than a plateful of warm cookies.

Reflecting on that experience, I see that throughout much of my parenting, I focused more on *doing for* than on *being with* my children. Many times this shame-based preoccupation with productivity interfered with respectfully listening to Dave and Becky with my undivided attention.

Perhaps our greatest obstacle to listening is our own desire to talk. Often we're like the man invited to give a brief talk at his Yale alumni meeting. Using the four letters in Yale as an outline, he waxed eloquent and long on each: Youth, Achievement, Loyalty and finally Enthusiasm. When he finished his "brief" talk nearly two hours later, a bored guest whispered to a companion, "I'm sure glad he didn't graduate from the Massachusetts Institute of Technology!"[1]

Our "talks" with our children may frequently become lengthy lectures or sermons. This is easy to understand when we consider that many of us grew up with parents who were "talk terrorists." While lobbing verbal hand grenades and detonating deadly word-bombs (often *very* sweetly), they taught us that parents possess the inalienable right to talk without listening. They made it as clear to us as their parents had to them: "Children are to be seen and not heard."

Now that *we* are the parents, we want to stamp our feet and shout,

"*My* turn, *my* turn!" However, our children have this annoying habit of wanting us to listen—*really listen*—to them. (Remember back when you still indulged that desire, before you surrendered it to inescapable barrages of parental verbiage—or perhaps to stone-silent stares?) This is a significant choice point for those of us longing to become shame-free parents. Will we "take our turn" and continue the family pattern? Or will we begin listening to understand with eyes and ears?

Here's something to consider when weighing this choice. First, some of us have begun to suspect that we don't understand our children much better than our folks understood us. Second, we learn more about our children by listening to them than by talking at them. If this is true, then we may discover our children more fully than ever before when we pay the price to become better listeners. The cost of this priceless discovery? We must willingly relinquish our turn at terrorist talking.

Another reason we need to listen to our children is to help them learn problem-solving skills. This may be 180 degrees from our own childhood experiences. In most dysfunctional families, when a child takes a problem to parents they tend to ignore it or "solve" it themselves by imposing their own ideas.

What a contrast to healthier families, where parents respond by asking something like, "What ideas have you thought of?" Parents then help their children generate and evaluate various solution options and potential outcomes. This process takes some time, and it requires that both the parents and the children listen, think and talk.

Talking vs. Not Talking

Well-functioning family environments are usually pretty noisy and interesting places with people talking, listening, questioning, laughing and so forth. Of course, there are individual differences in verbal expressiveness among family members. But even the least verbal person knows that talking is enthusiastically encouraged.

In these families anybody can talk about anything, but that doesn't mean everybody hears about everything. For example, it is unhealthy for parents to discuss explicit details of their sexual struggles with their children, but it is extremely healthy for these parents to talk about it with each other so that they can work toward improvement. This is not denial. It is respecting appropriate intrafamily boundaries.

Children may not always *want* to talk to their parents about everything, but in well-functioning families they know that they *can*. We encourage our children to talk not only by listening to them, but by using questions and comments that open them up rather than shut them down. For example, listen for the difference in the following parent-child conversations.

Example 1.
Fourth-Grader: "We had long division at school today and I got kinda confused."
Parent: "Kinda confused?" Or, "That didn't feel very good, I bet. What did you do?" Or, "Kinda confused? What did that feel like?"

Example 2.
Fourth-Grader: "We had long division at school today and I got kinda confused."
Parent: "Why didn't you ask your teacher for help?" Or, "Don't bother me, that's your problem. What do you think we pay teachers for?" Or, "I told you you're never going to be an astronaut."

Any of the first parent's responses invites a child to talk more about the experience. This parent could even have used the old standby, "I'd like to hear more about that." The child would still get the most important message: *having* a problem does not mean you *are* a problem, and you and your problems are important to me.

How eager would you be to continue this discussion with the

parent in the second example? Imagine how much *less* eager you'd be if you were only nine or ten years old. Since the second parent's responses are far more typical of shame-based families than the first, it is small wonder that these families are often "verbally impoverished."

"Nobody talked to anybody else in my family—we just didn't talk," Bill explained to his church's support group for adult children from dysfunctional families. "Oh, I don't mean we didn't speak words, I mean we never actually sat down and talked about real stuff."

The "real stuff" in hurting and hurtful families like Bill's is often pretty painful. Besides, no one wants to be guilty of violating the "Be Quiet" rule. This is how one woman described these silent family systems.

Silent Family

Something happened to me when I was just a kid.
It was a family member, but I can't say what he did.
I took responsibility for all he did to me,
But we don't talk about it, we're a silent family.

We must maintain the status quo.
What will our friends think if they know?
We've got to keep it hidden, so
Don't talk of it to me!
We must protect our family name.
We'll teach our kids to do the same.
We cannot face the sin and shame:
Our silent family.[2]

Does that sound anything like your family? If so, you probably grew up surrounded by secrets.

Surprises vs. Secrets

Surprise birthday parties and Christmas gifts can be delightful family fun. Well-functioning families often enjoy such surprises, but they are "allergic" to secrets. Secrets cause families to break out in shame—and even *more* secrets.

There is a huge difference between family surprises and family secrets. Surprises include eagerly anticipated and predetermined dates for "show and tell." It's great fun when Dad and daughter shop for a gift to surprise Mommy on her birthday. It is an entirely and devastatingly different matter when Dad masturbates in front of daughter and calls it "our special secret that would upset Mommy if you tell."

Creating secret-free families where open, honest communication is valued and modeled is one of the most effective ways to protect our children from abuse. Of course this means we must not involve our children in even the "small secrets" we routinely overlook. It's so tempting to instruct a child, "Don't tell Dad (or Mom) about this parking ticket," but it also is very confusing when we've told the same child not to keep secrets.

Yes, creating safe, straight-talking families can seem nearly impossible when we've cut our teeth on secrets and denial. It requires ruthless commitment to truth, often in the face of family pressure to "stop causing trouble." Here's more on this subject from the "silent family" we met earlier.

I just want someone to tell me what he did was wrong.
And I don't think it's good to keep a secret for so long.
I wish someone would validate the harm he did to me.
But we don't talk about it, we're a silent family.

The kinfolks say, "Forgive, forget.
Why do you have to mention it?
You're making way too much of it.

Why don't you let things be?"
We must protect our family name
We'll teach our kids to do the same.
We cannot face the sin and shame:
Our silent family.[3]

Clearly, not all family secrets involve hands-on abuse. It could be Uncle Joe's imprisonment, Grandma's mental problems, Mom's eating disorder, Dad's workaholism or a million other human infirmities which a family perceives as shameful. All family secrets are born of shame—that sense that we are not good enough but we must look perfect and problem-free. Curiously, one family's open knowledge may be another's secret shame.

I know a forty-year-old man who, literally, risks his life to protect the family secret: his adoption. Alan is seriously ill and his doctors have told him that it would be useful to have as much information as possible about his family history. Here's how he describes his predicament.

"About twenty years ago I accidentally discovered my adoption papers, but my folks had never mentioned it to me. I don't know why, but they didn't. Now there's just my mom and I'm afraid it would kill her if I tried to discuss it. If she had wanted me to know, she would have said something by now."

Alan's lethally loyal statement expresses not only the binding power of secrets, but their "power base": the common dysfunctional family myth that parents (and often other adult relatives) are so fragile that we children must shield them from truth—forever. Alan believes that myth; in fact, he's betting his life on it.

About now you may be ready for more suggestions about changing verbal communication patterns you heard and learned as a child. One mother developed an interesting formula. First, she would ask herself what *her* parents would do or say in a certain situation with her children. And then she did the exact opposite!

For those of us who value more explicitly biblical guidelines, I have another idea.

The "Truth Sandwich"

The Bible emphasizes the awesome power of words. Proverbs 18:21 even attributes the power of death and life to our words. Norm Wright does a good job of applying this and other key passages to the parent-child communication issue in *The Power of a Parent's Words* (Regal Books). To this resource and others, I want to add a word picture that captures for me the heart of biblical communication for all of us parents.

A few years ago I was meditating on the Ephesians 4:15 phrase "speaking the truth in love." Because I tend to think very visually, I "saw" a *truth sandwich*—truth "sandwiched" inside two layers of love.

The Ephesians 4:15 "Truth Sandwich"

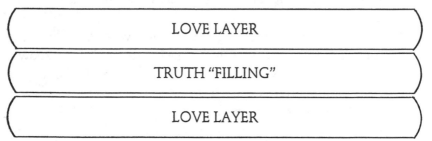

LOVE LAYER

TRUTH "FILLING"

LOVE LAYER

Figure 9-1.

Do you see it? Can you hear it? Just imagine how different our conversations would be if we were committed to conveying truth (as opposed to perpetuating family myths) and if we nestled that truth between layers of love. As you can see, we would begin and end with affirmations of our esteem and affection for the recipient of the truth sandwich. I've found that usually even the toughest truths are palatable when tucked within genuine affirmations of worth.

Example 1. Father to fifth-grade son consistently failing to complete his homework:

LOVE LAYER: "Jeff, I hope you know how much your mom and I love you. We think you're a really special guy."
TRANSITION: "So . . .

TRUTH FILLING: We're concerned about your not finishing your homework assignments lately. Let's talk about it." (Ideally, son and father would discuss the problem and work out a solution.)
TRANSITION: "Sounds like this will work, Jeff, and always remember . . .

LOVE LAYER: Mom and I love you very much. We know you're learning to work out problems like this on your own, and we want you to know that we'll be here to help you do it."

Example 2. Single mother to high-school senior daughter arrested for drunk driving:

LOVE LAYER: "Even though we've had some pretty wild arguments, Angie, I want you to know how much I love you. I'm sure I haven't said that enough in the past few years, but it's always been true. I love you and you are very important to me. You are so bright and have such potential. That's something else I haven't said often enough. Anyway, I want you to know that you are very special to me.
TRANSITION: "That's why . . .

TRUTH FILLING: I am not going to bail you out this time. I thought I was doing the best thing for you those other two times, but now I realize I wasn't. You need to go into the teen rehab program, Angie." (Ideally, mother and Angie would continue to discuss this serious problem. But let's say that Angie won't listen and screams, "I hate you for doing this to me.")
TRANSITION: "Yeah, you probably do. I'm going to be hoping and praying that you won't hate me forever, because . . .

LOVE LAYER: I love you very much. In fact, Angie, I want you to know that nothing you do will make me stop loving you."

When delivering truth sandwiches, the transitional word connecting the layers is critical. *Always use "AND" type words; never use "BUT."* Connecting two thoughts with "and" or similar words like "so" or "because" conveys that the second thought flows from the first. If we use "but," we set the second thought in contrast to the first ("I like you, but . . ."). When we're talking on serious subjects with significant people, like our children, we want them to know that our "truthing" (the literal Greek used in Eph 4:15) flows from our loving/caring. Above are two examples of truth sandwiches. You'll notice that the more serious the situation and the more "distasteful" the truth filling is likely to be, the thicker the layers of love need to be.

Obviously we don't need to use "truth sandwiches" in every verbal exchange with our children. However, knowing how to use them helps us feel better prepared to handle the inevitable serious problems that come. And on a broader plane, this concept suggests using twice as many affirmations as confrontations with our children.

Of course, to nurture our children, parents must do more than *just talk.*

Communicating with Touch

My husband believes that most research studies merely confirm common sense. This certainly seems to be the case with a recent study suggesting that nurturing touch is an extremely important and beneficial form of parental communication.

But this confirmation of common sense is not necessarily comforting to parents raised in dysfunctional families. In fact, touching is, dare I say, a very "touchy" subject with many of us. Perhaps examining some of the benefits of communicating with nurturing touch will motivate us to face some of the barriers.

Benefits of Nurturing Parental Touch

The recent study followed up children thirty-six years after first determining which of them had outwardly affectionate parents. This research found that *parents' physical affection and warmth toward their child correlated strongly with closer marriages and friendships, along with better mental health and successful careers in the child's future.* The principal researcher offered two explanations:

> Children may have learned the behavior [warm, nurturing relating] from their parents and be using it as adults. They may also develop a sense of security from this base of affection that enables them to go through life in a happy and healthy way.[4]

What remarkable support for the power of parental modeling and the common-sense "folk wisdom" that children thrive on lots of cuddles and hugs. Incidentally, this study found that the *most* successful and happiest adults received physical affection from their *fathers* as well as their mothers.

Imagine: as parents we have the power in our hands—literally—to increase our children's present and future well-being. What an astounding privilege! And what a terrible tragedy when barriers prevent or pervert it.

Barriers to Nurturing Parental Touch

A "safe-touch famine" is ravaging children across this land. "Safe-touch starvation," in one of two forms, afflicts most children raised in unhealthy families. And, as some of us know only too well, both create barriers to warm, nurturing touch when *these* children have children.

No touch: First, there are some families where children grow up with virtually no experience of their parents' skin against their own. This was Warren's situation, I learned. "I'm positive my mom or dad must have held my hand crossing a street or something, but I just can't remember anything like that. They never touched my sister or each other either, so at least I don't feel singled out," Warren said.

Some family and ethnic heritages forbid physical displays of affection. Disregarding a child's natural need for cuddling, this kind of heritage shapes a parenting philosophy that says tenderness "weakens" children, whereas coldness and severity strengthen them and better prepare children for real life. Warren's parents grew up with this belief and so they molded their children as their parents had molded them.

Warren shattered the family mold when he married bubbly, openly affectionate Belinda. It didn't take him long to adjust! Now he wants to be more physically expressive with his young children, so he's working hard in counseling and at home to stop old patterns and choose better ones.

Bad touch: A second type of "safe-touch starvation" exists in the presence of hands-on contact between parents and children. There is plenty of parental touching, all right, but it is anything but safe for the children. And it is impossible to exaggerate the damaging impact of this unsafe touch—physical and sexual abuse—on these children and their children.

In the worst cases, some adult children repeat sexualized and/or brutal touching with their offspring. However, many more abuse survivors avoid or minimize physical contact with their children to prevent such repetition. With all-or-nothing thinking, these parents conclude that the only way to avoid *abusing* their children is to avoid *touching* them. They are motivated by fear-tormented love in the service of their children's protection. Sadly, their children are apt to perceive only parental rejection.

Mothers who are incest survivors encounter particularly painful barriers to providing abundant nurturing touch for their children. For example, a mother may become very uneasy after observing her husband's affectionate physical contact with their daughter. This mom might even accuse her husband of being "too familiar" or inappropriate when his actions are clearly nurturing and completely nonsexual. Nearly every incest survivor I have counseled struggled with this. And, as some of us have discovered, these struggles usually intensify when daughters reach the age at which their mothers were sexually abused.

I always loved watching Garth wrestle and rough-house with both of our kids, the three of them tumbling on the living room floor in a hilarious jumble of arms and legs. But I asked Garth to stop wrestling with our daughter as soon as she had her first menstrual period. Garth didn't understand my request and thought it was pretty silly. But, assuming I knew more than he did about raising a girl, he honored it.

At the time, I didn't understand it either, especially considering that Garth's physical contact with both children had always been totally appropriate. All I knew was that, for some unknown reason, it was very important to me.

My puzzling request made sense a few years later when the previously repressed memory of my step-uncle's sexual abuse burst into my awareness. *He molested me the summer I had my first menstrual period.* The unsafe sensation I felt when I saw Garth on the floor with Becky was a ghost from my past. Unknowingly, I robbed my daughter by creating a barrier to some of her physical nurturing.

We just can't escape the truth that allowing Jesus, the Great Physician, to do his healing work in us is one of the most loving things we can do for our children. As we experience more wholeness, we will be able to nurture our children better through healthier talking and touching.

Personal Reflection

On a scale of 1 (disastrous) to 10 (glowing), how would you evaluate the communication "health" in your childhood family? How about in the family you helped create for *your* children?

To help you decide, consider the following:

☐ Did/do parents' words deal death to children's good feelings about themselves, their potential and their dreams, or breathe life into them?

☐ Did/do parents listen to their children with *eyes* and ears?

☐ Did/do parents provide lots of cuddles, hugs, gentle touching of faces, affirming pats on shoulders and heads and so forth for their children?

The healthiest parents respect age-appropriate changes in the form and frequency of the physical contact their children want. For example, young children enjoy holding their parents' hands or sitting on their laps in public. Older children and teens would be humiliated by the same actions.

☐ Were/are children safe from hands-on harm?

This question may be more difficult to answer accurately than we might think, because the more we were abused as children, the less likely we are to recognize child abuse! (Chapter eleven provides practical help for this double-bind dilemma.)

Looking Ahead

"Experts" say that communicating our feelings helps to connect us, whereas communicating only thoughts—especially judgments— tends to isolate us. This is not particularly encouraging for parents raised in unhealthy families where feeling and expressing emotions violated the "Be Numb" rule.

In the next chapter, we'll see how this emotional numbness affects our parenting and what we can do about it.

10
We Can Learn to Feel Good About Feelings

*I*n my family, feelings were a luxury we couldn't afford."

That's how one very bright, sincerely committed Christian woman described the emotional environment in her childhood home with an alcoholic father and a physically abusive mother.

As a child, this woman could not let herself fully experience the confusion, terror and despair she felt at the hands of her abandoning and abusive parents. Her emotional numbness was a lifesaving friend. Now, as an adult, she does not deeply experience *any* feelings, even pleasant ones. Having outlived its protective purpose, the old "friend" turned against her and became a life-flattening foe.

We don't need to be survivors of such devastating hands-on abuse to have problems feeling and expressing our emotions. Even far less dysfunctional families often enforce an unwritten "Be Numb" rule that their adult children continue to obey throughout life. As a result, some of us feel guilty because we occasionally experience strong emotions, especially sadness or fear or anger. We may call such experiences *losing it* or *breaking down* or *falling apart.* I call them *being human.*

Emotional Nature vs. Family Nurture

Feelings are not troublesome childhood conditions we are supposed to outgrow like measles or acne. Yet many of us seem to believe that we are more mature if we never display strong emotions. Disowning our emotions does not make us more mature—it makes us less human.

God created us with the capacity to experience a full range of pleasant and unpleasant emotions. Ecclesiastes 3:4 portrays this broad panorama of our emotional nature as it describes "a time to weep and a time to laugh, a time to mourn and a time to dance." Of course Jesus is our supreme example of perfectly balanced human functioning. And since Jesus authentically and appropriately expressed a full range of emotions, including great joy, deep grief and intense anger,[1] we can assume that God wants us to follow the same pattern. Why don't we do so?

Something seems to have happened to many of us on the way to adulthood and full emotional functioning. The biblical pattern described above was crushed and constricted to fit the needs of the impaired and consistently overwhelmed parents who headed our unhealthy families.

If we grew up in *extremely* hurting and hurtful families, we probably learned that strong emotions are dangerous because they lead to verbal violence or physical battering. I know a lovely Christian woman I'll call Joan who is terrified of anger—hers or other people's. Throughout childhood Joan saw her father express his anger by kicking in doors, punching holes in walls, abusing family pets and occasionally striking her mother. Concluding that anger and all strong feelings are dangerous, Joan sought safety in emotional numbness.

Joan was victimized by what is termed "vicarious abuse." Her father never physically abused her, but Joan clearly recalls living daily in the fear that "next time it would be my turn." Sadly, multiplied thousands of children grow up in families where their "turn" comes all too often, usually as an expression of an adult's anger. No wonder such children learn virtually nothing about *appropriately* expressing anger. As adults, they believe there are only two choices when it comes to feeling strong emotions like anger: either "clam up" or "blow up." As we trace their early experiences and perceptions, we can see how adult children from battering families arrive at emotional numbness.

We don't have to be from such obviously unhealthy families to have learned to sacrifice our God-given emotional nature on the altar of personal safety. In far less hurtful families we may be taught that strong feelings are embarrassing betrayals of emotional weakness and self-indulgent signs of personal and spiritual immaturity.

Perhaps we repeatedly got messages like "big boys don't cry" and "only sissies are afraid of the dark." And of course there is that ever-popular refrain sounded in hurtful families for generations immemorial: "If you don't stop crying, I'll really give you something to cry about!" What an unmistakable message that *parents* have the ability and the right to determine what should bring their *children* to tears.

Eventually these children get the message that it is safer to let important adults, like parents and pastors, tell them what to feel rather than to respond authentically to their own emotions. After all, if we hear "you shouldn't feel that way" often enough, we start to believe it. So we deaden and deny our authentic feelings, and we learn to check our relational environment for clues to the officially approved emotion of the moment.

Emotional Robbery in Christian Families

Jesus came to take away our sins, not our feelings. Yet some Christians seem to believe all strong emotions are wrong. Others act as if believers are called to "fake it for Jesus' sake."

Maybe this explains why many Christians "put on a happy face" in every circumstance of life—even when other emotions would be far more honest.

Certainly, I lived most of *my* Christian life believing that I would be "a bad witness" to non-Christians if they ever saw me cry or frown. Somewhere along my faith journey I was taught that "real Christians" are constantly joyful and that such an emotional state would be irresistibly winsome to unbelievers. In effect, I was operating from the belief that my "happy face," rather than the Holy Spirit of God, had the power to make someone a Christian.

We may struggle with such burdensome misbeliefs about emotions even if our parents were sincere, churchgoing Christians, like my mother. Undoubtedly our parents simply taught us the emotional misbeliefs taught to them by *their* parents and other spiritual authorities. These misbeliefs usually include most of the following:

(1) conflict is *always* harmful and *totally* avoidable;

(2) anger is *always* sinful so we must *never* be angry;

(3) fear is *always* sinful and feeling it disqualifies us for God's service; and

(4) Christians should *always* be happy and "nice."

Many of us still live as if those statements were true in spite of Jesus' example in the Gospels and other passages of Scripture which say otherwise.[2] For example, Jesus didn't *always* avoid conflict, and he was *not* very happy or "nice" when he angrily pronounced scathing rebukes upon the Pharisees or drove the money-changers from the Temple. In addition, God mightily used the apostle Paul even though he admitted being so afraid he trembled. (See 1 Cor 2:3.)

Furthermore, God seems to assume that his children will *not* always be happy when he has Paul tell Roman believers to "rejoice with those who rejoice, *weep with those who weep*" (Rom 12:15 NRSV). In fact, why should we be surprised that living in a sin-stained world brings *at least* as much weeping as rejoicing? Yet many of us feel guilty when we don't skip and giggle our way through pain-lacerated lives.

I know Christians who have been criticized for grieving the death of a child or spouse "longer than they should"—as if their sorrow were lack of faith. For example, several years ago Charlotte's infant daughter died while her family attended a "Be Numb" church. After a job transfer and move, Charlotte finally sought counseling.

"Jeff and I were like statues after we lost our baby. She lived twenty hours and she was gone. Somehow we got the impression at church that Christians aren't supposed to grieve since we know we'll see her again," Charlotte told me. "I am beginning to realize how unnatural it was to display almost no grief whatsoever over our baby's death."

Between stifled sobs she added, "Maybe worst of all, we didn't let our older two children discuss or mourn their baby sister. It probably sounds stupid, but we honestly believed we were being very spiritual and setting a good example."

Charlotte's misbelief about sorrow is not unusual among Christians in "Bible-believing" churches. These churches seem to believe the highest emotion-related value in life is the "take-anything factor," that is, the ability to endure any experience whatsoever without betraying the slightest hint of emotion other than happiness. After all, for years they've been singing that Christians are "happy all the day." Apparently these churches develop their concept of human emotions more from a hymnal than from the Bible.

Scripture does *not* say we should never grieve the dead. Rather, in 1 Thessalonians 4:13, it urges Christians to grieve *differently* from unbelievers who "have no hope." Sadly, Charlotte's church and many others twist this verse to buttress their unhealthy "Be Numb" rule and its corollary: "Happiness is holiness." As a result, adults in such congregations forfeit authentic and appropriate sorrow (and other "unspiritual" emotions) to earn their church's "seal of approval."

Moreover, this unhealthy, unscriptural concept is passed along to another generation. And the unsuspecting children have no way of knowing that they are being robbed of their emotional nature just as their parents were robbed a generation before. Thus the shamed become the shamers—again.

Choosing Healthier Emotional "Rules"

We likely will continue this intergenerational emotional thievery unless we deliberately determine to do it differently. As always, we must make new, healthier choices about our own emotional lives before we can help our children with theirs. This means recognizing and challenging the beliefs that form our "emotional guidance systems," and then reclaiming the emotional nature we may have self-protectively relinquished.

Until we honestly assess our beliefs about emotions we won't know what does or does not line up with biblical truth. The list in figure 10-1 will help us recognize the truth or error in our beliefs about feelings.

But recognizing our basic beliefs about feelings is only the first step in choosing healthier emotional expression. We also must confront our misbeliefs and their underlying "lethal logic."

Challenging "Lethal Logic" About Feelings

By now we realize that our misinformed beliefs about feelings have come more from dysfunctional family dynamics and demands than from a biblically informed respect for our God-designed emotions.

Scriptural teaching about feelings declares that all human beings have

(1) a God-given array of emotions that we can experience authentically, and

(2) a God-given responsibility to express these emotions appropriately—without harming others and sinning.

Therefore, we need to study Scripture to learn what appropriate emotional expression is, and we need to rely on God to energize our

Recognizing Beliefs About Emotions

Shame-Bound Lies	Shame-Free Truths
1. Emotions are unnecessary, bothersome, un- spiritual and embarrassing. I need to work on eliminating them in myself and my children.	1. Emotions are a gift from God and an inte- gral part of our human natures which reflect his image.
2. Emotions are bad and dangerous, so it is safer when I avoid them and teach my chil-· dren to do the same.	2. Emotions are neither good nor bad. They can be expressed appropriately, and I can learn to do that and model that for my children. I and they are less fully as God created us when we avoid feeling emotions.
3. If I begin to feel my emotions, I will "lose it," "fall apart," "go crazy" or hurt someone— maybe even my children.	3. When I am able to feel my emotions, I will become more authentic and alive. Recognizing and expressing emotions may feel strange and scary at first, but I can find "appropriate emo- ters" to help. I don't have to hurt anyone.
4. It is stupid to get all upset over things that happened years ago. It is best to "let sleeping dogs lie." Besides, none of that affects me or my children now.	4. It is appropriate for children to feel con- fused, afraid, sad or angry when their parents neglect or abuse them. Those feelings did not go away just because I had to learn to disown them. They are still inside, affecting my life and my parenting today, and it is best to face them and feel them honestly.
5. When I felt sad as a child, no one was there for me. I couldn't stand to feel that despair and loneliness again. Besides, my children will think I am weak if I let them see me cry or display sadness.	5. I have resources now as an adult that I did not have as a child. I can find more reliable (but imperfect) human comforters. And I know (or can know) God personally and have his comfort. It will be painful to grieve child- hood losses, but I can stand it. Besides, I will be teaching my children to authentically, ap- propriately grieve when they see me doing it.
6. As a child, I was told I should never be an- gry. I just know God is angry about my anger, both my anger about the past and about pre- sent situations. Besides, good Christian parents never admit they feel angry.	6. It is appropriate to feel angry about what angers God. Misleading or abusing children angers God. I can learn to express my anger appropriately and without sinning (see Eph 4:26). When I do this, I'll be teaching my chil- dren to express anger appropriately.
7. As a child, I learned that I was a "sissy" or a "coward" if I was ever afraid. And my church seems to teach that really good Christians are never afraid. I don't want my church or my children to think I am a sinful sissy, so I will do whatever it takes so that I never feel fear or any other "unapproved" emotion.	7. It is natural and human to be afraid of peo- ple and situations that have harmed or can harm us. God seems to have made provision for this unpleasant human emotion by repeat- edly encouraging us in Scripture to trust his power and presence in our fears. When my children see me honestly face and feel my fears and choose to trust God anyway, they will be learning a very valuable lesson.

Figure 10-1.

efforts to live what we learn.

In contrast, what I call the "lethal logic" of unhealthy families says that all human beings have

(1) an innate capacity to be perfect and problem-free (this includes feeling happy at all times), and

(2) an innate capacity to totally avoid "bad" feelings like anger.

Therefore, no one in our perfect, problem-free family (or church) ever experiences "bad" feelings, so we don't need to waste time talking about them or teaching our children how to express them in healthy ways.

Eliminating Unwanted Feelings

The natural extension of this lethal logic tells us we are emotionally defective whenever we experience "unapproved" feelings, because we've been taught that good people (especially good Christians) never have bad feelings like anger or fear. So we determine to eliminate the unwanted bad feelings as quickly and effectively as possible when they threaten to break into awareness. We undertake this impossible task with a creative assortment of reality-bending defenses: deadening, disowning, distracting, disconnecting from and defining away our "unacceptable" emotions.

Deadening our emotions with legal or illegal, evangelically acceptable or unacceptable mood-altering substances temporarily tricks us into believing we can actually become the emotionless robots some of our families and churches seek. This is one reason addiction to mood-altering substances is pandemic in families that enforce the "Be Numb" rule. This is also why, for example, it is more acceptable to be life-threateningly obese than to be obviously unhappy or "not nice" in shame-based church families operating from the "lethal logic" mentality. Following this unbiblical approach, many Christian parents teach their children to emulate their examples by, literally, stuffing their emotions with high-fat and sugar-laden foods. *We may have found ourselves automatically doing this with our children if eating is the only emotion-management skill we learned growing up.*

Disowning our "bad" feelings by attributing them to others rein-forces whatever emotion-flattening effects the deadening substances provide. When we're skilled in the disowning defense, we say lots of things like, "You make me so angry," or, "I'm not scared. You're the one with the fear problem."

Distracting ourselves with constant activity effectively numbs our emotions and, in many cases, simultaneously wins approving smiles and fatter paychecks. This particular defense is doubly seductive for us hard-core approval addicts. We certainly don't want to risk disap-proval by experiencing any "bad" emotion banned by our families or churches, so we are desperately seeking effective emotional blockers. We are apt to use deadening and disowning to some degree, but we really get "hooked" on distracting because it packs a two-part payoff. First, we stay too busy in our outside worlds to pay any attention to what's going on inside of us emotionally—or in any other way. And second, we get approval "fixes" when people say, "I just don't know how you manage all that you do at church with your busy family and your job," or perhaps, "You work more hours than anyone we've ever had in this plant. I wish all our employees had your work ethic."

Disconnecting from unwanted emotions is usually the only defense available to very young children. So, if we experienced severe, trau-matic abuse at an early age we have probably developed the ability to detach our inner selves from what's happening around us as soon as we begin to feel anxious, scared or angry. (Of course we don't *know* that we have felt anxiety, fear or anger and protectively have chosen to disconnect; we just do it automatically.) We may begin to view the threatening situation as if we were on the ceiling looking down at it. Or perhaps we "go away" into an inner world where we feel safe.

Defining away our "bad" emotions can become a defense of last resort if someone happens to notice telltale flickers of feeling in us.

This emotion-denying ploy is popular among Christians raised with the "Be Numb" rule. When using this defense, in effect we redefine the "unacceptable" emotion out of existence. This is how it sounds: "No, I'm not angry—a little frustrated perhaps, but not angry." Or, "Afraid? Of course I'm not afraid. I'm just concerned."

Do any of these defenses sound familiar? If you're like me, you've probably dabbled in all of them to some degree. Once we recognize our feeling misbeliefs and the defensive lifestyles they foster, we must choose to reclaim our God-given emotional heritage by changing our beliefs and increasing our feeling skills. As we do, we can share these truths and skills with our children, whatever their ages.

Increasing Feeling Skills

It isn't surprising that most of us from shame-based, emotion-flattening families lack the two most basic feeling skills: accurately recognizing our feelings and appropriately expressing them. No wonder we haven't known how to teach our children to feel good about feelings.

Let's take a closer look at these skills with the goal of learning so we can live and teach them.

Recognizing feelings: Increasing this skill means dismantling defenses that may have become "trusted protectors" because they have helped us obey the "Be Numb" rule and feel safe. In fact when we feel emotions today, many of us experience nothing more than an unrecognizable physical sensation—a vague kind of inner "buzzing" that we deaden with our "drugs" of choice as soon as possible.

My favorite numb-ers are (1) "performing" (giving more seminars or media interviews) for approval—preferably *immediate,* and (2) eating—preferably *chocolate!* That's why I tend to gain weight and burn out when I'm under stress. That's also why I must *decrease* my use of emotion-numbing defenses before I can *increase* awareness of my emotions. And so must you.

Decreasing our numbness: I believe that numbing ourselves with substances or activities is an attempt to self-medicate the pain of living. These emotional anesthetics keep us from experiencing painful feelings and from facing the painful history behind those feelings. Remember, *emotions have a history.* Unless we have given ourselves permission to know the truth about our yesterdays, we won't risk feeling authentic emotions today.

However, all self-medicating addictions have the same distressing side effect: they wear off! This means we must continually repeat and gradually increase our dose to get the desired results. Eventually we may find ourselves organizing our daily lives around the numbing activities or substances. If we miss a dose, we become more aware of the inner buzzing and feel agitated and anxious. And in especially stressful times that stir unwanted feelings, we usually increase the dose.

Most of us have seen or heard enough about alcoholism to recognize this progression. But we may be alarmed to discover this same pattern in our uses of food, sleep, television, shopping, work (paid or volunteer—including at church) and a host of other possible emotion deadeners.

If we need to feel intensely painful emotions, we may need the support of Christian professionals or pastoral counselors as we choose to decrease our numbing. When we begin to experience the effect of this choice, we are on the way to the second part of feeling recognition.

Increasing our awareness: Each of our bodies responds to specific feelings in a unique way, sometimes called a "feeling fingerprint."[3] When we grow up in troubled families, we usually become skillful speed readers of other people's feeling fingerprints while remaining virtually illiterate about our own. This may be one reason why, for example, we explode with *enormous* anger; we can't read our bodies' signs of *building* anger.

Think of a recent situation you recognize as frightening, relaxing or whatever. How did your body signal your fear, your relaxed feeling or other emotions? What did you experience (tightness in your jaw or shoulders, slower breathing, deep sighing)?

If you can't answer these questions, you may need to ask a different one: what do others see? Ask trusted family members and friends to provide feedback on your feeling fingerprints. Our adult children are apt to be especially eager helpers here! As we increase our feeling awareness, we can teach our children this skill. (Be prepared for resistance and resentment in older children.)

For example, when we notice that a child's body language signals strong feelings, we can mention it gently. This might sound like, "I notice your cheeks are red and you're clenching your jaw. What are you feeling inside?" Also, when our children express their emotions, we can help them increase feeling awareness by asking questions about their feeling fingerprints. "Where is your body feeling the 'scared'?" or "How does your 'so happy' feel inside?" are examples of possible questions.

This second suggestion presupposes that our children know how to put their feelings into words. At this point, we've moved into the second feeling skill area: expressing.

Expressing Feelings
Many of the books listed in appendix C explore appropriate emotional expression. For example, in chapter nine of *Released from Shame,* I give eight specific suggestions to increase our repertoires of healthy emotional expressions, and we can use almost all of them with our children. We'll examine here one example of shame-bound feeling expressions and two examples of shame-free.

Shame-bound feeling expression: Arlene is a beautiful Christian woman in her early thirties. She recently entered her second marriage and was considering going off birth control pills. "I know my husband wants to start a family as soon as possible since neither of us is getting any younger," Arlene said in our first counseling session. She went on to explain her uncertainty about having children by describing a recent visit with her family.

"My sister was yelling, 'Stop crying or I'll really give you something to cry about,' at her little boy as she spanked him over and over. It was just part of the chaos I've come to expect every time we kids go to our folks' place for the holidays." Arlene shook her head slowly as she told me how upset she felt when she heard her sister's words, because their alcoholic father had physically abused them both as children. And the only thing more certain than their mother's failure to intervene in the beatings was their father's slurred recitation of his I'll-really-give-you-something-to-cry-about speech.

"You'll never believe what my dad did," Arlene said. (Actually, it wasn't difficult at all.) "He tried to stop my sister by telling her that that was what *his* father always said to *him*. 'Well, where do you think I got it from? I learned it from *you*,' my sister yelled back at him." Arlene paused and added softly, "My dad has absolutely no clue that he treated us kids the way Grandpa treated him. I am so scared to have kids—scared that I won't see some of the rotten stuff I learned and so I'll just pass it on to *my* kids too."

Arlene came for counseling to learn how to recognize and change shame-based and unhealthy family patterns, including those that shape our expression of feelings. I was pleased that I could honestly assure Arlene that her goals were both biblical and attainable, even for someone raised in a family as abusive as hers.

Shame-free feeling expression: Thirty-something, bright-eyed Rowena became a Christian four years ago. She too was raised with an alcoholic father, and so was her husband. Rowena acknowledges that she still has a long way to go in her recovering journey, but she has leaped giant obstacles as surely as Superman ever did. Rowena is a wise and loving parent working diligently to "do it differently" with her children.

Rowena's parents were too distracted by their own problems to respond sensitively to their children's feelings, but she is determined to improve *her* children's emotional environment. For example, she has taught her two daughters to ask for hugs when they need some extra comforting. Shortly before she gave birth to her baby boy, her younger daughter climbed into what remained of Rowena's lap and asked for a hug.

Rowena asked the four-year-old if she was worried about Mommy's having enough hugs to go around after the new baby came. This led to a talk about God's love for *all* his children and about how mommies' and daddies' "love supply" gets bigger with each new baby. This interaction is so different from what occurs in most dysfunctional families where children are called "selfish" or "babyish" for expressing such a natural need for reassurance of their parents' love.

It is one thing to "do it differently" when we are alone with our children, but we've graduated into the big leagues when we can maintain our shame-free parenting in the presence of other adults.

When Rowena learned that her nine-year-old daughter needed a tonsillectomy, she went to the largest Christian bookstore in town because she wanted to know how to emotionally support her daughter. One of the things Rowena learned in the books was that it is appropriate for children to cry when they experience pain. This is how Rowena told the rest of the story.

"Shortly before Christy's surgery, a nurse came to insert an I-V needle in her arm. Just as the needle was about to go in, Christy's little lip started quivering, so the nurse began a speech about, 'Oh, be brave and don't cry—you've been so good so far,' and a bunch of other stuff that sounded like something my mother would have said. I looked right at Christy and said, 'Honey, it's really okay to cry if it hurts. That's natural and Mommy does it too.' I could tell the nurse didn't like that by the look she gave me, but she didn't say anything.

"I feel really good that I did that. In the past, if someone was inappropriate with my kids, I either didn't notice at the time or was too 'chicken' to say anything. So later I'd tell the kids to disregard what they heard. This was the first time I've been able to stick up for one of my kids right when I needed to. I praise God for guiding me and giving me the courage I needed."

Did you notice how the nurse's response resembled those typical of impaired parents? The nurse's focus was on her own desire for a hassle-free needle insertion. She totally disregarded her young patient's natural fear and pain response. It would have been so easy for Rowena to slip back into accepting such disregard for a child's feelings. But she didn't. And if God will help Rowena learn and teach her children to feel good about feelings, he will do it for us.

Personal Reflection

Briefly describe how the people named below handle(d) the emotions listed: how do (did) they express them or what do (did) they do to numb them?

Sadness:
My parents

Me

My children

Anger:
My parents

Me

My children

Love:
My parents

Me

My children

What intergenerational patterns did you discover? What changes do you want to make? How will you make those changes? When will you begin?

Remember, you cannot change anyone but yourself. But when you *do* change and begin consistently living healthier feeling beliefs, you will profoundly influence your children.

Looking Ahead

When she intervened to protect her daughter, Rowena was responding to an emotional boundary violation by the nurse. This was an extraordinarily healthy action for someone raised in a shame-based family with its blurred boundaries and loose limits. We'll take a closer look at other boundary issues next.

11
We Can
Learn to
Like Limits

*G*ood fences make good neighbors," writes poet Robert Frost, and I suspect he is correct. In the same way, limits, or boundaries, help to make healthy families.

For those of us raised in unhealthy families, appropriate personal and family boundaries may be as mysterious and unfamiliar as smoke detectors to an aborigine. Smoke detectors are extremely useful; they are just not part of a aborigine's world.

In this chapter we'll examine four of our major boundary-setting challenges. You may discover some "ghosts" from your nursery. If what you're reading is hauntingly familiar and discomforting, take heart: these memory phantoms cannot harm you today. However, they may pinpoint childhood episodes you mistook for dead and gone when, in fact, they were buried alive.

How Boundaries Work

Appropriate family boundaries help to provide a sense of safety and stability for all family members—especially for the children. Healthy boundaries around and within families are neither too permeable, allowing everything and everyone in, nor totally impermeable, creating walls that keep us isolated. Appropriately permeable boundaries *around* families give members a special sense of "us," without creating a fortress mentality toward the rest of the world.

Within families, boundaries are like doors in a home. Some are almost always open or closed, and others swing in or out in response to family changes. For example, in healthy families, there need to be appropriate boundaries between the parents and the children. Parents perform certain family functions that *never* include their children, such as expressing affection sexually. In my opinion, this should occur between parents behind closed (and locked) doors—literally.

Other boundaries between parents and children may shift appropriately over time. For example, it isn't wise for parents to share details of their financial struggles with young children. However, this boundary door often swings open gradually since talking to older offspring about family finances is usually appropriate.

In addition to boundaries between the family and the outside world and between parents and children within the family, each family member has a *personal* boundary that establishes where he or she ends and another person begins. We are not born automatically knowing how to establish or recognize appropriate personal boundaries. And some are easier to distinguish than others. For example, we actually see *physical* boundaries (this is where my body ends and yours begins). Others, like *perceptual* boundaries (these are my perceptions and observations and those are yours) or *emotional* boundaries (my feelings are mine and your feelings are yours), are invisible.

It is unrealistic and inappropriate for me to expect you to perceive the world exactly as I do, or to feel just exactly as I feel about every situation—just as it would be for me to demand that we occupy the same body! But such expectations do occur. They may be called obedience, loyalty, respecting your elders or even submission to authority in dysfunctional families (and churches).

We must learn to value clear limits/boundaries before we can teach them to our children. And we may need to return as "defective" much of what we learned about boundaries in our childhood families.

Setting Boundaries for Our Children: Discipline

"Don't be afraid to discipline your child; it is critical to his self-image. By setting rules and expectations, you teach him to respect society's limits."[1] So speaks Berry Brazelton, M.D., professor emeritus of pediatrics at Harvard Medical School.

"Discipline your son, and he will give you peace; he will bring delight to your soul." So says Proverbs 29:17.

Most of us would agree that children behave better when they know what is expected of them and know that their parents are consistent in rewarding and punishing. Wise and loving parents will discipline their children. Well, that settles *that* boundary issue. Or does it?

A closer look reveals that most parents raised in hurting and hurtful families struggle with one of two equally ineffective disciplining styles.

Overcontrolling Discipline

Harshly authoritarian parents attempt to control their children through verbal and/or physical dominance. Usually this approach continues an intergenerational pattern of abuse in the name of not "sparing the rod."

As we've seen in earlier chapters, verbally violent parents use name-calling, ridicule, unfavorable comparisons and a host of other wounding words with their children. In addition—and to our sorrow—many of us have used *verbal threats* purposefully to control our chil-

dren. Here are two types of abusive verbal threats many of us probably heard as children and may have used as parents.

1. *Threats of abandonment* are a form of verbal and emotional abuse,
not appropriate discipline tools. Statements like "If you don't come
with me right now, I'll leave without you" are designed to frighten
a child into hurrying to match a parent's pace. Abandonment threats
can terrify young children. Instead of using this natural fear against
a toddler who plops down on the floor, we could say something like
"Either you come with me now or I'll have to take you by the hand
and make you come with me." In this case, we must be prepared to
pick up the child and carry him or her with us if necessary.

2. *Nonspecific, menacing threats* are harmful because they capitalize on
our children's vulnerability. In addition, using statements like "Do it
or else" or "Do that again and I'll cram my fist down your throat"
actually undercut our parental authority because (in homes without
hands-on abuse) our children know these are empty threats. Such
empty but menacing threats invite children to push harder to see
where their parents *will* set limits. It is far more effective to set
appropriate limits which we will actually enforce.

Tragically, some parents *do* employ physical abuse as discipline:
confinement in closets, beating with coat hangers, boards, belts, fists.
Often these parents were "disciplined" with such abusive treatment
as children. Recent research suggests a possible link in this devastatingly destructive chain of intergenerational child abuse.

Several studies required subjects to judge physically abusive and
physically punishing vignettes. The results showed that "subjects
who experienced the same treatment as portrayed in the vignette
perceived the discipline as less severe, more appropriate, and were less
likely to label it as abusive than those who had not experienced the
same treatment."[2]

This is another vivid example of research that supports common
sense. In limit-setting terms, this translates to: "If our folks did it to
us and we survived, it's all right to do it to our kids." Sadly, even some

churchgoing and apparently Christian parents specialize in physically abusive overcontrolling, mistaking it for biblical discipline. If we grew up in these families, we probably don't know any other options.

But overcontrolling discipline has an opposite extreme as well.

Undercontrolling Discipline

Standing in a mall beside a child who is screaming, "I hate you for not letting me [whatever]!" is not one of parenting's bright spots. And there's a very good chance that at some point we will hear statements like that when we attempt to set appropriate boundaries for our children.

No parent enjoys being the target of his or her child's anger, but for those of us raised in hurting and hurtful families, it can be absolutely intolerable. We may have looked to our children to provide the loving acceptance we've always longed in vain to experience. And in infancy, they seemed to meet our needs for unconditional love.

Then, as they developed and required boundaries, many of us couldn't tolerate the agony of our children's anger, even though Scripture warns parents to expect that response.[3]

Our children soon learn to hold us hostage with their copious tears, angry frowns, declarations of withheld love. If we regularly give in to these tactics, we betray greater concern about keeping our children's approval than about building their character.

Incidentally, we approval-addicted and appearance-preoccupied parents are sitting ducks for our children's *public* misbehavior and tantrums! Our kids will figure out pretty quickly that we are more concerned with looking like perfect parents to avoid shame-based embarrassment than we are with enforcing appropriate behavior. But this situation is not incurable, as Gina discovered.

Gina came for counseling to deal with personal pain from growing up with shame-based and unrealistically rigid, demanding parents. She also longed to improve her parenting skills. Gina explained that kindergartner Timmy especially "bulldozed" her in public until he got what he wanted.

When I asked Gina what she was thinking and feeling at those times, she replied, "It's as if I stop functioning like a responsible adult and a reasonably effective parent to Timmy. I sense everyone looking at me disapprovingly and I feel like a stupid little kid. [I call that "growing down."] I just want to make Timmy shut up even if I have to buy him every toy or candy bar in the entire store."

As Gina began to change personally, her parenting changed too. I suggested she use some of the following ideas to manage Timmy in public.

1. Just before entering a store or restaurant, remind your child of a few simple rules like: "Stay with me, talk in your 'indoor voice' (that is, without screaming) and look but don't touch without asking." *Remember, good discipline begins with clear instruction.*

2. When rules are broken or need to be created on the spot, take the child aside, preferably to a distraction-free area.

3. If a child is screaming and out of control, go immediately to the most remote area of the store and stay there until you reestablish control. (The faster you interrupt the child's tantrum momentum, the better.)

4. If this is a new way of managing the situation, your child will probably expect you to cave in as usual. He or she likely will continue the unacceptable behavior at first. If this is the case, take your child outside the store or restaurant and walk around or sit in the car until things improve. As a last resort, go home.

One parent observed that abandoning a shopping cart of groceries or a table of restaurant food to regain control over a child may seem drastic, but it pays off in the long run. He once removed his six-year-old daughter from a restaurant and sat in the car with her until the rest of the family had finished eating. Then they went home. He concluded that the minor inconvenience was well worth the lesson it taught his daughter.[4] (This same parent suggests that, for emergencies, we can carry a fake nose-and-glasses set. If all else fails, we approval-addicted parents can put it on and retreat into anonymity!)

Both the overcontrolling and undercontrolling discipline extremes are born of overwhelming insecurity about ourselves as parents. Both fail to communicate self-control to children. In appendix C, you'll find several books listed which offer better, more biblical methods of child discipline.

Even when we conquer this challenge of appropriate boundary setting *for* our children, we still face the struggle to maintain healthy boundaries *with* our children—so they can *be* children.

Maintaining Boundaries with Our Children

"Where have all the parents gone?" asks Boston *Globe* columnist Ellen Goodman. She eloquently laments the increasingly widespread "adultification" of children by parents who unburden themselves by burdening their children as they force them into confidant roles more suited to spouses or adult friends. Goodman describes two females on a streetcar, one sharing her troubles and the other listening. They were mother and daughter. However, the one seeking understanding was the adult, and the one extending it was the ten- or eleven-year-old child.

Goodman concludes:

I am not a fan of rigidity or of distant authoritarian parenting. *But I see a great many pseudo-sophisticated children who need parents, not tall pals.* They need to believe that grown-ups can solve their own problems, that adults are helpers, that parents are emotionally stronger. *That is the point, after all, of growing up.*[5]

I cringe when I hear a parent describe a child as his or her "best friend." If this parent is married, he or she is actually committing emotional adultery against the spouse by perpetrating emotional incest upon the child. Ideally, our spouses are our most intimate, trusted confidants and best friends.

It won't be easy to break that pattern, especially if our marriages are troubled or have ended by divorce or death of a spouse. It is so tempting to turn to our children to fill emotional and companionship needs. They are conveniently available, and we may even believe they "owe it to us" because we have so many more problems than they. But this is an inside-out, upside-down reversal of healthy, biblical family patterns where children *supply* needs and parents *fill* them.

Does this mean we cannot share all of our concerns with our children? Indeed it does. Children's narrow shoulders were never designed to carry the weight of a parent's deep needs and fears. We must find other sources of comfort and counsel. *And we must purposefully give our children permission to be children.* Why is this child-protecting boundary setting so difficult for many of us? Perhaps because we must face the truth and the pain of "the great childhood robbery."

It is a crime to murder or rape a child, but it is not against the law to steal a childhood, and childhoods are stolen perhaps millions of times a day. Crazy as it seems, the more we were robbed of our childhoods, the more we tend to rob our children of theirs! If our parents behaved like "tall children" and expected us to function like "short adults," we are apt to do the same with our children.

Again, we face the bitter truth that breaking this pattern means forfeiting our "turns" at childhood stealing. I agree, it isn't fair to have to be responsible, honest-to-goodness grown-up parents when we didn't really get to be carefree kids. But that's the price for "doing it differently" with our children.

Sometimes we are not the only ones who want to "do it differently" with our children.

Boundary Setting with Our Parents

"Love is better the second time around," according to an old song title. Many adults raised in unhealthy families discover that their *parents* want to use their *children* to prove that parenting is better the second time around. A twofold boundary-setting struggle results.

First, we may need to loosen boundaries. Our children often enjoy visiting with our parents even when the grandparents are only "consistently adequate." **And if** our parents have changed and grown into kind, godly people, they enrich our children's lives enormously with their wisdom and nurturing love. Curiously, this blessing for our children often represents a painful emotional battle for us. We may be envious of the warm attention our children get from two people who failed to give us enough when we were children.

But what if our parents are still subtly or blatantly abusive and "consistently inadequate"? Are we obligated to allow them to visit our children? These questions raise the second boundary-setting issue with our parents: when we need to tighten up.

Tightening Up

Let's just admit up front that this is a difficult and painful issue. On the surface, it seems only right that grandparents have access to their grandchildren, especially when they are like those of a little boy I heard about recently. After church this boy's mother asked how he had liked his Sunday-school class. He told her he'd had a new teacher. When his mother asked who it was, he answered, "I think it was Jesus' grandmother." Barely stifling her laughter, his mother asked how he had come to that conclusion. "Well," the boy replied, "all she ever did was show us pictures of Jesus and talk about him!"

Sadly, not all grandparents are doting, picture-toting types who lavish unconditional love upon their grandchildren. Pretending otherwise is dishonest and dangerous. Yet pretending that people and situations *are* something they are *not* is second nature to most of us raised in unhealthy families. And that can be very unhealthy for children, for—amazing as it may seem—many parents regularly expose their children to hands-off and even hands-on abuse perpetrated by grandparents. These parents never consider monitoring or ending this painful pattern until they recognize it is wrong. And that isn't easy.

Annette carries inner scars from her childhood with an emotionally distant, perfectionistic mother and a harsh, verbally and emotionally abusive father. "I love my folks and I believe God has given me the grace to forgive them, but I absolutely dread being around them because of how Daddy is," Annette told me. "Tell me if I am being too sensitive. That's what my mom and older brother say. Maybe they're right. But I worry about my son being hurt by Daddy like I was."

Annette recounted the latest family gathering where her father, as usual, sliced and diced everyone present with his scalpel-sharp tongue. When Annette intervened to protect her six-year-old son, her father ignored her and increased his verbal assault on the child, adding "Mama's boy" to his arsenal of wounding words. Annette described what happened next.

"My husband was outside, so I had no emotional support. My brother said I was too sensitive, which is what I heard from my folks every day when I was a kid. And my mother said the same thing she's been saying for as long as I can remember: 'Well, that's just how Daddy is.' I think she almost fainted when I said I didn't think that was a good enough excuse anymore. Maybe it was okay when I was a kid getting his garbage mouth dumped on me, but it isn't good enough for my son. Daddy may be that way forever, but that doesn't make it right and it doesn't mean that I have to keep acting like it is."

Annette took her son outside and asked her husband to take them home. Since he had grown increasingly uncomfortable about his father-in-law's incessant verbal abuse, Annette's husband strongly supported her choice. Annette's mother phoned the next day demanding that she apologize for "disrupting the family's special time." Her brother called the following week and told her she was "acting like a spoiled brat."

"At this point, I'm not sure about when or if I'll visit my folks again. But I know for sure that it hurts being an outcast in my family," Annette said.

I know other parents who have chosen to severely curtail and closely monitor, or even end altogether, their children's contact with grandparents. For example, Jan's alcoholic mother refused to refrain from drinking when Jan let her two children visit. "When I learned about my mom driving the kids to get burgers, I went wild!" Jan said. "I had asked her not to drive with the kids when she was drinking, but she totally ignored my request. She insisted that I was making a 'big deal out of nothing,' just like she always does about her alcoholism. I know the kids love her and she loves them. And I love them all. But I will never let the kids spend the night again or even visit without me there. And if she is drinking, we'll leave immediately."

At this point, Jan has the legal right to set tighter boundaries with her mother. However, the situation is changing.

Grandparents' "Rights"

Grandparents' rights groups have lobbied for and won "visitation rights" with their grandchildren in all fifty states in cases where the grandchildren's parents are divorced. Extending grandparents' power even further, in 1991 a New York court granted visitation to a grandfather whose grandson's family was intact.

Is it the court's place to mandate intergenerational family relationships? The attorney who founded the "Grandparents' Rights Organization" says it is.

> Children should have the right to have shared memories and experiences with their grandparents . . . and the opportunity to experience that kind of unconditional love. If this experience is being denied because of the death of a grandparent, that's a tragedy. If it's because of family bickering or vindictiveness, that's an injustice.[6]

If parents object to dangerous behaviors or verbal/emotional abuses by their children's grandparents, is this appropriate child protection or is it "vindictiveness"? It is appalling to contemplate a day when parents would lose their boundary-setting ability to the relatives who can afford to hire the most competent lawyers and to whom legislators have granted the most "rights."

A grandparent's loving relationship with grandchildren is not an inalienable right to be enforced through judicial power. It is a precious privilege earned through a loving and respectful relationship with one's own adult children. Furthermore, just as loving our children is not sufficient in and of itself to make us consistently adequate parents, just loving their grandchildren does not automatically make grandparents adequately trustworthy. Scripture describes people who "love in words only" yet whose deeds are not loving. Jan's mother repeatedly proclaimed that she loved her grandchildren—*and she really does.* Sadly, for her and her grandchildren, her love has neither magically cured her alcoholism nor made her trustworthy.

If for some unimaginable reason I should ever become hurtful to my granddaughter, I would want my son and daughter-in-law to protect her from me. Their top priority would not be protecting some illusion that I was still a trustworthy and safe grandparent; *their top priority would be protecting their child.*

I am not saying, though, that parents' rights are sacrosanct and irrevocable. Tragically, some parents are irresponsible and unsafe. Sometimes grandparents are forced to look on in horror as their own children and/or their children's spouses neglect and even abuse their grandchildren. If you are one of these grandparents, I beg you to make your grandchildren's safety the top priority as you decide whether or not to intervene on their behalf.

Our minor children's and grandchildren's safety must always be the top priority of all parents and grandparents. And this priority is indispensable and nonnegotiable in the realm of sexual boundaries.

Boundary Setting and Sexuality

All parents from hurting and hurtful families face similar sexual boundary-setting challenges, in one sense. Yet some of us face additional struggles.

Experts in dysfunctional family issues often note that we adult children do not know what a "normal" healthy family looks like. Our struggle to recognize and replicate healthy family characteristics is especially vital and difficult in the arena of sexuality.

We may be comfortable asking "what's normal" regarding communication or even child discipline, but not usually when it comes to sexual matters. I know adults raised in unhealthy and sexually unsafe families who assume it is normal to have a father who leaves pornography around the house, forbids his daughters to close their bedroom doors or insists on using the toilet while his adolescent children bathe. These are violations of children's sexual boundaries.

Parents should model modesty, the need for appropriate privacy and healthy sexual boundaries. And their children's modesty, privacy needs and sexual boundaries should be respected, not ridiculed as often happens in unhealthy homes. Indeed, God created all things beautiful and we are "wonderfully made." But I believe it is inappropriate for parents to walk around unclothed once their children pass toddlerhood. I don't mean you have to panic and scream if a kindergartner sees you getting dressed. You can teach appropriate sexual boundaries both by the way you function typically and by the way you respond to an unusual circumstance.

Clothing, closed bedroom and bathroom doors, and having one's own bed are all appropriate sexual boundaries within families in our culture. So is refusing hugs and kisses—even from grandparents and other relatives. We need to support our children's rights to "just say no," even at Grandma's house or at the church. *Never force your child to accept touches he or she does not want!* (Medical and dental care are excepted.) When we do, we inadvertently make a child more vulnerable to sexual boundary invasions.

A Special Challenge
If we were sexually abused as children, especially in an ongoing family setting, then as parents we face painfully difficult issues regarding our increased vulnerability to sexual boundary invasions.

Research studies report that mothers of incest survivors often are incest survivors themselves. Apparently, having learned to survive as young girls by trivializing or repressing (unconsciously forgetting) their own sexual boundary violations, these mothers may unknowingly expose their daughters to similar abuses. If their abuse memories are still repressed, these mothers don't recognize their tendency to screen out the signs of potential perpetrators' inappropriate attention to their daughters.

In addition, *if sexual-abuse-survivor parents still operate from a "shame grid," they may fail to protect children from known perpetrators even when they remember the abuse.* When interpreting their early experiences through a perceptual filter woven from shame and magical thinking, child victims conclude that the abuse occurred because of something wrong in *them,* not because of something wrong in their *abusers.* Later, as parents, these abuse survivors must get help to reinterpret their childhood experiences more accurately and attribute one hundred per cent of the responsibility for the abuse to the perpetrators. Without this new "truth grid" these parents will still see their abusers as basically good, safe people. And since these survivor parents usually see their own children as sweet and innocent, they assume those "basically good and safe" abusers would never hurt such sweet and innocent little children.

This tragedy waiting to happen is compounded by the fact that most sexual abuse perpetrators are trusted authority figures, not the "stranger danger" types we may be more likely to warn our children to avoid. As a result, *we may actually expose our children to the very same trusted authority figures who sexually abused us years before.*

Helping an Abused Child

Learn to recognize signs of sexual abuse which can tell you what your child may be unable to say. Read appendix A, which lists indicators of sexual abuse. If you suspect your child has been abused, or if you get "bad feelings" reading appendix A, please don't just dismiss this painful subject. Tell your child what you see that concerns you. Gently remind the child of your love and desire to protect him or her if anyone is being hurtful. Pray for wisdom and sensitivity, and make extra efforts to keep communication lines open with this child.

If a child tells you she or he has been abused, *believe it and take action.* (If your child is too young to talk, and if appendix A confirms your worst fears, take action also.) Gently ask "how" and "show me" questions. *Never ask "why,"* because it may sound like an accusation. Never minimize with statements like "It's no big deal, this happens to lots of little girls and boys." And don't say, "That's not so bad, something like that happened to me when I was a kid too." My mother used the second response when, at fifty-one, I finally told her about the sexual abuse by my step-uncle when I was eleven.

The following steps will get you started in the direction of helping and healing.

First, call the police and/or child protective services. *Child abuse is a crime—not a family's "dirty linen" that we don't air in public!* While you wait for an officer or social worker to come and complete a report, listen and talk to the child as calmly as possible. Abused children need to hear reassuring messages like:

☐ "I believe you."
☐ "It's not your fault."
☐ "I'm sorry that happened to you."
☐ "I'm glad you told me about it."
☐ "We're going to get some help."

If the abuse just occurred, do not wash the child or change any clothes. All states have standard procedures for handling sexually abused children. Often this includes taking them to a hospital emergency room. Assure the child that this treatment is not punishment for being bad but is done to help him or her feel better.

Studies suggest that parents' reactions to a child's report of abuse may be more significant than the experience itself in determining how well she or he recovers. If you know or suspect that you were sexually abused as a child, you and your child will benefit if you *both* get counseling from specialists in sexual abuse treatment.

I am certainly *not* saying every incest survivor's child will be molested. And I am *not* trying to create an atmosphere of sexual distrust within extended families. Nevertheless, appropriate sexual boundary setting is absolutely essential in healthy families. Children aren't born knowing how to recognize these boundaries, so parents need to model and teach about them. This is extremely difficult if we don't know what appropriate sexual boundaries are or how to perceive past or impending violations.

We must learn to recognize our own and our children's sexual boundary violations, for surely such abuses are among the darkest of the "deeds of darkness" which God urges believers to completely avoid and thoroughly expose. (See Eph 5:11.)

Personal Reflection

Do you recognize yourself as an undercontrolling or an overcontrolling parent? If so, will you read, talk to healthier discipliners or get other help to change your disciplining style? When will you start?

Do you see some evidence that you have been expecting your children to listen to your problems, give you advice and fill your life so you won't be lonely? List several more appropriate sources for getting your needs met.

How can you begin appropriating these sources so your children can be children? When will you start?

If you have not done so already, please read appendix A. Do you see a cluster of these indicators in your child or any child you know? (Remember, just one or two do not necessarily indicate sexual abuse.) Will you get help for that child/children? (Remember, you can report child abuse anonymously in most states.)

Do you see a cluster of adult indicators in yourself? Will you give yourself permission to tell the "secret" and get help at last? Please do it. You are worth it. But even if you can't do it for yourself, do it because it will make you better able to protect your children.

Looking Ahead

In this chapter we've explored some very serious issues. Yet even when we escaped hands-on abuse, growing up in a hurting family is seldom a laugh fest. That's probably why many of us raised in these families take such a deadly serious approach to ourselves and all of life. And we usually don't know how to have fun. We'll *work* on that in the next chapter!

12
We Can Learn
to Have Fun
(If We Work at It!)

*T*hou shalt not commit fun!"

This rendition of the dysfunctional family's "Eleventh Commandment" turned our church-based support group into a veritable comedy club of one-liners about our childhoods in fun-deficient families.

Yet for many of us raised in these unhealthy families, this is no laughing matter. We really are *not* very skilled at relaxing, having (or being) much fun or enjoying family traditions and holiday celebrations. In fact, some of us aren't entirely convinced these are worthy pursuits for either children or adults—especially if they are Christians. Others of us recognize the value of relaxing and of developing and observing pleasant family occasions; we just don't know how.

These overly serious attitudes were not genetically determined by some grimness-carrying chromosome. It's just that growing play skills and relaxation appreciation in shame-based families is a little like raising roses in the Sahara. If we want to be increasingly shame-free parents, we need to rethink our attitudes about personal relaxation, family fun and celebrations. Play is a very important ingredient in a healthy life—our child's life, yes, but our own as well.

Relaxing Is Not a Sin

Several years ago Tim Hansel wrote a delightful book entitled *When I Relax I Feel Guilty.* That pretty well says it for a lot of us, doesn't it? We've heard about the health benefits of relaxing. We may even read entire books about relaxing. It's just that when we actually practice relaxing, we feel, well, *guilty.* And shame-full. At least, that has been my experience.

I love Chopin's piano compositions. I enjoy playing several of the simpler ones and listening to the more difficult pieces flow from the fingers of gifted pianists. Yet only in the last few years have I been able to listen without a twinge of guilt. I kept hearing the echo of my mother's words when, as a child, I occasionally sprawled on my bedroom floor to relax and listen to a classical music radio program. She said, "You should be doing it, not just listening to it!"

"You should be doing it" became the guiding motto of my life. And, believe me, I became a doer. It seemed that busyness was next to godliness in my childhood family, and later that personal productivity priority meshed well with Garth's highly-honed work ethic. Our union had an extremely high grimness potential!

Fortunately for our children, my delightful, fun-loving mother-in-law taught her son to value creativity and play as well as work. So Becky and Dave saw Garth as a "fun dad." Sure, he sometimes exploded with anger and often had to travel and work very long hours, but when it was time to play, Garth was a "fun dad." He even had play skills: he could invent games, ride a bicycle, roller-skate.

In contrast, I possessed *none* of those play skills. Oh, I knew how to cook and bake, clean house, sew and run a Vacation Bible School, but I didn't know how to be a "fun mom." I could never seem to give myself permission to do anything so blatantly unproductive as sit down and play with Dave or Becky. That seemed like an inexcusable waste of time.

I could not relax any more comfortably than I could play. Growing up before anyone warned us about the harmful effects of deep suntans, I looked forward to sunbathing weather wherever we lived. But I never just lolled in the sunshine to enjoy its relaxing warmth. That would have been too unproductive. I always took at least one book with me so that I could read something enlightening or inspiring, rather than waste time just relaxing (or reading fiction)!

In the past few years, I've met many other adults who share my struggles with relaxation deprivation and fear of fun. As I've thought about our similar backgrounds in shame-based families, I think I may have identified the underlying misbeliefs we must change before we can give ourselves permission to enjoy our children and our lives.

Fun Phobia

From earlier discussions you may recall that shame leaves us feeling uniquely flawed—as if there is something wrong with us that is not wrong with anyone else on earth. Consequently, we believe we are hopelessly different and "worth-*less*" than others. The resulting sense of what I call *existence guilt* provides the shame-shaped foundation for the overserious, joyless lives many of us lead.

"I feel guilty for existing because I don't deserve to take up oxygen and space on this planet." This is the heart-cry of existence guilt. Others deserve to exist, so they have the right to relax, have fun and just *be*—but not the shame-bound. Since we feel guilty for being alive, we must constantly be *doing* to earn the privilege of *being.*

From this shame-based perspective, our productivity is our only reason and justification for existing. So the more we do, work and produce, the more secure we feel. As a result, *on some deep level we may perceive resting and relaxing as actually life-threatening.*

What's more, many shame-based families reinforce existence guilt as children learn they are "lazy," "useless" or "wasting time" if they aren't busy with homework, household chores or highly organized activities (usually selected by their parents). If this shame-based lesson is taught with physical as well as verbal abuse, these children likely will feel panicky and paralyzed when they attempt to relax and have fun as adults. Henry knows that feeling only too well.

Henry, a quiet Christian in his late thirties, works hard to create a healthier family than the one in which he was raised. Recently, he identified one of the barriers on the road to that goal. Henry grew up on a small farm with an extremely demanding, physically abusive father. On those rare occasions when his father caught Henry resting, the boy carried welts and bruises for weeks to remind him that he was "worthless and lazy." Henry is beginning to see how that crippled his capacity for relaxation.

"Last Saturday was really a scorcher, so I took a break from mowing the lawn to have some lemonade and watch my kids and their friends run through the sprinkler," Henry told his Christian counselor. "As soon as I sat down on the porch steps I started feeling nervous and jittery inside. I know it's crazy, but I felt really guilty and didn't want anyone to see me. Then I remembered that that was exactly how I felt as a kid when I was scared to death my dad would catch me loafing."

As Henry and his counselor continued their work, he began to give himself permission to "be" without having to "do" every moment. Recently, Henry said, "I still hurt inside when I see my children play, because I never knew how to play or relax. But I am getting better. I can actually sit and relax now—at least for a few minutes."

As a recovering workaholic and practicing relaxer, Henry is making purposeful changes to end his family's intergenerational legacy of existence guilt. Unfortunately, most Americans are not following this path.

According to Diane Fassel, author of *Working Ourselves to Death: The High Cost of Workaholism and the Rewards of Recovery,* "There's this belief that we are nothing if we're not constantly active and busy, and that's not going away." A major element in workaholism's lethal legacy, according to Fassel, is "parents passing on to their children workaholic values, shuttling them from place to place and never allowing them to just play and be kids."[1]

Similarly, many of us shame-bound Christian parents pass on to our children the idea that God is vaguely or violently displeased when we are not working from sunup to sundown. Often, we teach and show our children that relaxing and playing are too frivolous and unspiritual for truly committed Christians.

Ignoring Physical Needs and Creativity

When we live workaholic lifestyles, whether expressed downtown in an office or at home and church, we hurt ourselves and our children in two ways. First, our children learn that human bodies have no need for rest and relaxation beyond minimum sleep time. This lie ignores the physical damage of prolonged adrenalin-fueled overwork.

In addition, when we insist upon "making every minute count" by squeezing productivity from all possible situations, we rob our children of opportunities to develop their creativity. For example, we are unlikely to stroll slowly with our children on a leaf- or rock-hunting expedition if we believe walking has to be race-speed to produce cardiovascular benefit or else it is a waste of time.

Similarly, when families focus solely on productivity, parents overlook opportunities to develop creativity. For example, we may think only of punishing our children when they make excuses for unfinished chores. But if we value creativity as well as responsibility, while insisting our children complete their tasks, we could allow some creative silliness first by encouraging them to come up with lots of imaginative and clever excuses, such as "I didn't do the dishes because there was a shark in the sink."

If this sounds like a ridiculous waste of time, perhaps you grew up in a silliness-is-sin type of family that short-circuits children's creativity. Inflexible families that rigidly insist children do things "just right" also stifle creativity. I once heard of a first-grade teacher who chided a little boy in her class for his response to the flower-drawing assignment. "Flowers don't have faces," she told him solemnly. "Mine do," replied young Walt Disney.

Apparently, Disney's teacher saw him as being "silly" or perhaps as "fooling around having fun" when he was supposed to be learning to draw flowers. Sadly, many of us may have responded similarly when our kids were "goofing off." We aren't apt to value unstructured play and fun times for our children if we rarely experienced them ourselves. And if we see our children as little "wild things" needing to be tamed and turned into trouble-free, low-maintenance and highly productive family members (as soon as possible), we likely will perpetuate our fear of fun.

But there is hope; we can move beyond our fun phobias. I know this personally and from many of the counselees I have seen. One of these, a lovely Christian woman, wrote to thank me for sharing some helpful truths during our counseling work together. She also enclosed a photograph her husband took of her playing dolls with their first-grade daughter. She said this was an example of how much her life had changed since she began to live by healthier rules than those she had learned growing up in an abusive family.

That's the place to begin—deliberately choosing new "rules" about fun. After we give ourselves permission to relax and have fun, we may discover we are "recreationally impaired"—we don't know *how* to have fun. Take heart; play skills such as flying kites, roller-skating or camping out in the back yard are simple enough for even us adults to learn. We may need help at first, but once we get the knack of having fun, we will eventually be able to relax and play even *without* our children's supervision.

Respecting Individual Preferences
Sometimes when we begin letting ourselves have fun and develop

recreational skills, we forget that our children are separate individuals with separate bodies, emotions and perceptions.

When Jerry was growing up he often begged his workaholic, businessman father to take him fishing. Jerry had developed a "love-at-first-bite" relationship with fishing after a friend's dad took Jerry and several other boys. However, Jerry's father disliked fishing and he refused his son's repeated requests. Now Jerry is a dad to a son and two daughters, and he has been learning about healthier personal and family living. He's also discovering the wisdom of respecting individual family members' play preferences.

"I kept taking my eight-year-old son, Joey, fishing with me because that father-and-son-fishing-buddies fantasy was my childhood dream," Jerry told his counselor. "I finally realized that Joey hated fishing and only went because he thought I'd be mad if he didn't go. When I talked to him about the whole 'play-thing,' Joey said he'd much rather camp out in the back yard together or go skating."

Some of the healthiest parents I know give their children opportunities to sample many recreational activities. These parents also respect each child's preference for different types of play and fun.

Once we leap the okay-to-play hurdle, we can expand this radical concept to developing family celebrations and traditions. Again, we can learn new, better ways of "being family" than we saw as children.

Celebrating Our Families in Special Ways
Any regularly repeated activity—productive or just for fun—can become a family tradition. I know a family that makes a ritual of cleaning house together on Saturday morning and then going out for a fast-food family lunch. Other families plan weekly picnics (on a blanket in the family room during bad weather) or a weekly family night at home that Mom and Dad schedule in their appointment calendars. These regularly observed rituals "anchor" family members inundated by tidal waves of individual busyness. In some households

these "anchor times" include a family meeting designed to let members air and resolve family problems.

Whatever form your family rituals take, remember that they are intended to provide regularly scheduled times for *relating*. This means that walking in the woods is more effective than window shopping in a mall. Watching a movie together will be effective only if you talk about it together afterward. Appendix C lists several books filled with creative suggestions for starting family traditions. One of the best is *Let's Make a Memory* by Gloria Gaither and Shirley Dobson.

I wish these books had been around years ago. But even without them, our family managed to establish several rituals that created delightful memories. For example, Becky and Dave remember the Saturday evening "taco tradition" when they were growing up. Every Saturday evening when we weren't at swim meets or elsewhere, I fixed tacos from scratch. Like many families, we often missed eating together during the week because of Dad's travel and the kids' activities, so that Saturday night supper was very special. Years later I learned that Dave and Becky looked forward to it all week.

Garth and I also established a family tradition of celebrating our children's entrances into adolescence. For their thirteenth birthdays, we redecorated their bedrooms in the styles they selected. We even bought new bedroom furniture that was all theirs (to take when they left home) in place of the hand-me-down pieces they'd had as children. They helped us with the painting and wallpapering. And both children understood clearly that they had to live with whatever decor they picked!

Bedtime talks with the children and special family vacations also became cherished traditions. Other important Wilson family rituals centered around Christmas. Tragically, in dysfunctional families the Christmas holiday season brings added chaos and even increased episodes of abuse. No wonder Christmastime often triggers a depressing, stomach-churning "holi-daze" for those of us raised in such families.

'Tis the Season to Be Jolly?

Christmas may bring *joy to the world* of many families, but in many others, drunken curses and cries of pain split almost every *silent night* of the season. One chilling statistic estimates that "450,000 women will be violently abused in their homes between Thanksgiving and Christmas."[2] Most of these homes contain watching, listening children experiencing vicarious abuse in the process. Still other children learn that *their* holidays are a painful "hellish-daze" symbolized more by black and blue than red and green.

Several years ago as I was just beginning to recognize and understand the impact of my childhood losses, I came face to face with some of my own "ghosts of Christmases past." As I watched one of those sticky-sweet seasonal commercials showing three generations of an impossibly beautiful family smiling impossibly brilliant smiles and singing carols around an impossibly glorious Christmas tree, I began to sob. I don't mean a sniffle or two. I don't mean eyes filling and spilling a few tears. I mean waist-deep, chest-heaving, right-out-loud sobs. I had never before felt my sorrow over the absence of loving family holiday celebrations. I remember childhood Christmases only as frighteningly chaotic, intensely stressful and painfully lonely.

With Christmas memories like these, we probably will have confusing, conflicting emotions during the holidays. And if we still insist on numbing the feelings connected to painful childhood memories, Christmastime signals an increased availability of all the seasonally sanctioned addictions. Alcohol abuse, overeating, overspending, overworking to earn gift-buying money and "overchurching" to earn approval from God, the pastor and the entire church family—all of these come to a cacophonous, crazy-making crescendo at Christmas . . . in the name of the Prince of Peace.

With the powerful pull of hurtful family patterns and childhood memories, we may be tempted to abandon our dreams of ever celebrating Christmas with "peace and good will." What's more, we usually feel guilty and extremely unspiritual for not sharing the Christmas joy other Christians seem to experience. As always, our struggles have histories rooted in the realities of dysfunctional family life. We need to recognize that. But we do *not* need to continue repeating it.

Reclaiming Christmas Joy

We can learn to enjoy the holidays if we are willing to evaluate our family traditions to distinguish the "keepers" from those that need to go. Here are six suggestions to guide this process.

1. "Purpose in your heart" to focus on the true meaning of Christmas, the coming of Immanuel—God with us. In Daniel 1:8 (KJV) we discover that the outstanding Hebrew young man Daniel "purposed in his heart" to honor God in a hostile environment.[3] When Daniel chose to focus on obeying and glorifying Jehovah God, all his subsequent choices were what my husband calls "no-brainers." In other words, Daniel didn't really have to use his brain to deeply ponder each option because he had already established his purposed focus. Once we have "purposed" that Jesus is the "reason for the season," we will have a framework for evaluating our holiday schedules.

2. Reevaluate your Christmas activities. Maybe your family could do this during Thanksgiving weekend. Don't automatically discard all your parents' Christmas traditions. Prayerfully sift them and retain those that fit your "purposed" focus. On the other hand, give yourself permission to be a "disloyal child" by celebrating differently from your folks or other family members. For instance, consider staying home for a more relaxed and restful Christmas celebration instead of traveling to one or both sets of grandparents. If you do, be prepared for shocked, critical reactions from the "more loyal" family members. Garth and I established this pattern from our very first Christmas because we had heard too many horror stories of the we-went-to-your-folks-first-last-year-so-it's-my-folks-first-this-year variety. We never regretted our decision.

3. *Borrow Christmas traditions from healthier families.* Talk with your healthiest friends at church or elsewhere about what they have found effective. Ask your own family for ideas too. Tailor your plan to your own family needs and preferences.

4. *Check your newspaper for inexpensive, enjoyable community activities.* Maybe you just want to take one evening to load everyone in the family car, hit a fast-food spot and then drive around looking at Christmas lights. Don't try to do everything, but do some things to have family fun. After all, Christ brought us joy!

5. *Create a family giving project.* This tradition captures the heart of Christmas: God giving us his very best possible gift—*himself in flesh.* Your giving project can be as simple or elaborate as you want to make it. For example, every year I baked about a dozen varieties of Christmas cookies. (Those were the days when I was a full-time homemaker.) The children would help me fix paper plates heaped with cookies, swaddled in plastic wrap and tied with red and green ribbons. Then they would go together to distribute them to neighbors and friends.

Many years we also "adopted" needy families by providing gifts, food or clothing. Becky and David have never forgotten the year we all drove to deliver a trunkful of canned goods and gifts to an impoverished family in an unbelievably ramshackle house. Our children had only seen pictures of such living conditions and could barely believe people, including children their ages, actually lived like that. As you can imagine, in the next few days we had lively conversations about social justice, welfare policies, the value of education, God's grace and a dozen other topics.

6. *Set limits on the number of family, work and church activities you and your children attend.* Don't immediately accept an invitation or responsibility simply because you have that day or evening free. (I still fall into this trap.) *Schedule some unscheduled time!* Quiet evenings at home during December are not symptoms of social ostracism. They can be refreshing oases in our deserts of frantic overactivity.

At Christmastime in churchgoing families, evangelical hyperactivity reaches a frenzy that can sap the peace and joy from the season. We really do not have to attend each and every Christmas activity listed in the December church newsletter. Really, we don't. However, if we are still actively approval-addicted and if we attend churches that judge members' spiritual maturity primarily by their attendance records, setting limits on church Christmas activities won't be easy.

Remember, our new, more Christ-centered family Christmas traditions are part of our larger value of arranging relaxing, fun-filled activities for ourselves and our children. And we can make this plan *work.*

Personal Reflection

If you were tried for being a "fun parent," would there be enough evidence to convict you?

If you lack play skills, will you purposefully attempt to learn some? (Remember, this will benefit you as well as your children.)

How will you do this? When will you begin?

Do you feel guilty when you relax?

Are you weary enough to consider giving yourself permission to disobey your parents' "be-productive-every-moment" rules and examples?

If so, list some simple, inexpensive ways you could begin practicing relaxing. (Examples: soaking in a warm bubble bath; lying on your back outside looking at the stars or the changing cloud formations; walking slowly while listening for birds and looking for pretty wildflowers, leaves or rocks.)

Do you have regularly scheduled family "rituals" that provide pleasant opportunities for relating together?

If not, are you willing to begin some? How? When will you start?

Looking Ahead

Earlier I described the family tradition we established to ceremonially mark our children's passages into adolescence. This family tradition was a kind of "releasing ritual," reminding us and our children that they were growing up and our family was changing.

In the next chapter, we'll explore the unhealthy family's resistance to releasing its children. We also will learn how we can gracefully allow our children to grow and leave home.

13
We Can Learn
to Give Wings
Not Strings

*I*t seems an unlikely comparison. *Yet according to Psalm 127:4-5, children are* like arrows. And from this picture we find some parenting clues.

First, ancient archers knew they needed to polish their arrows. They did so to rub off any irregularities that might prevent an arrow from accomplishing its intended purpose. In a sense, we "polish" our children when we discipline them and when we set appropriate boundaries to teach them responsibility and respect for God, for legitimate authority, for themselves and for other people.

An arrow also needs to be balanced so that its flight is straight and true. And healthy parents recognize that we must balance child discipline with encouragement, affirmation and clear messages of parental love.

Arrows need to be polished and balanced, but they also need to be

pointed in the right direction. Tragedies occur when arrows fly hap-
hazardly. Similarly, we need to point our children onto right paths
by teaching and modeling biblical values and by consistently and
prayerfully exposing them to the message of God's gracious, redeeming love.

Parenting tasks such as communicating by talking and touching,
teaching about God and setting boundaries parallel the archers' prep-
arations of their arrows. Yet both archers and parents have one remaining task of supreme importance. Even when arrows and children
have been polished, balanced and pointed in the right direction, they
must be *released.*

In this chapter we'll explore the challenge of releasing our children—gradually giving them wings by letting them go to be fully
responsible for themselves, their decisions and their lives. Let's begin
by examining some reasons why parents often attach strings to the
child-releasing process.

Truth-Based Resistance
We may drag our feet a little on the path to our children's emanci-
pation even when our families are reasonably healthy and shame-
free.

First, consistently adequate and loving parents can expect to feel
both joy and sorrow as we anticipate our children's growing up and
going away from home. Garth and I genuinely enjoy our children's
company. We knew we would miss them when they left for colleges
many states away from us. Simultaneously, we were delighted to see
them seek appropriate independence and shoulder the accompanying
responsibilities it brings. In retrospect, I think we helped ourselves
and our children when we openly discussed this ambivalence.

Second, even in basically healthy homes, parents sometimes fear
they haven't prepared their children sufficiently for "real life" away
from the cozy family nest. As a result, we may experience some
emotional tussles as we anticipate releasing our children. I know I did.

Because Dave was such a responsible and godly young man, I firmly believed he would make consistently sound moral decisions when he was thousands of miles away at college. And he did. However the summer after his high-school graduation, I suddenly realized I hadn't taught Dave how to sort dirty clothes and do laundry. How would he survive without this critical skill? I resolved this releasing crisis by conducting a crash course in "Laundry 101" for both children.

Reflecting on my behavior that summer before our first child left home, I've concluded that all the unrecognized fears about my inadequate parenting suddenly coalesced to produce that intense laundry-tutoring reaction. Yet, in view of the world into which we launch our children, a certain amount of release-related fear is not unwarranted. This raises the third reason many basically competent parents resist letting their children go.

Scripture declares that "the whole world is under the control of the evil one [Satan]" (see 1 Jn 5:19). Sincere Christian parents often fear that our children won't be able to withstand the world's decidedly dangerous voices, values and vices. Even if we trust God's love for our children, we might not trust our children's love for God. As a result, we resist the releasing process each step of the way.

Depending on local situations, we may be right to worry about handing over our young children to secular school systems. Christian schools or home-schooling networks often are wise options. But despite the real and present darkness of this world, we eventually must release our children to live their own lives away from home and away from our protection.

Each of these parental resistance scenarios contains a kernel of truth that legitimizes our releasing struggles. This isn't surprising, since consistently adequate parents focus on confronting reality as truthfully as possible in substantially shame-free families. However, shame, not truth, shapes parenting behaviors in unhealthy families.

Shame-based Resistance

First, if our parents never really supplied wings by giving us permission to live our own lives, *we may believe that this is how families are supposed to function.* In shame-based families, impaired parents attach strings to their children by teaching them to feel disloyal and "uniquely bad" (the essence of shame) for seeking independence. Sometimes "tall children" parents use shame-strings to create "short adult" children, as we saw in chapter eleven. Curiously, this shaming pattern's flip side teaches the lie that "respecting your elders" and "loving your parents" mean letting them control your life forever—just as if you were still a young child. But you're not!

You have grown and changed, and healthy parents recognize and reward such God-designed human development by progressively letting go of their children. Unfortunately for many of us *and our children,* the child-releasing pattern we learned from our parents is far more "keep them grown down" than "help them grow up."

Loss of Love

A second powerful motive for keeping children grown down is our shame-based fear of abandonment. If I believe a child is my primary or sole source of unconditional love, I won't readily relinquish his or her infant-intense dependency. This is especially true if, on some deep level, feeling unloved and abandoned appears to be the only alternative to keeping my child in a state of newborn neediness. (Remember, shame says I don't deserve to exist and I will be abandoned unless I am needed to *do* for others.)

I believe this is the major unrecognized reason that many parents who are divorced or in unhappy marriages resist their children's steps toward adult independence. They feel as if their "love supply" will disappear if their children need them less and leave for lives of their own. Frequently, the *youngest* child feels the "strings attached" most intensely. This was Janeen's experience.

"The night I got engaged, my mom burst into tears and talked about how hard it was going to be to lose her 'baby,'" Janeen told me. At thirty-five, Janeen is a devoted wife and mother of two girls who struggles daily to maintain her adult priorities and resist the tar-baby tenacity of her mother's "sticky" shaming. Janeen described her youngest-child role as "the last buffer between my folks in their bombed-out marriage."

Loss of Power

While many mothers and fathers resist letting go of their children because they fear abandonment and loss of love, others primarily seem to fear loss of personal power in the family. Personal power includes such elements as openly acknowledged ability to master tasks and reach sound decisions, a sense of personal competence and the like.

Most dysfunctional homes operate on a "power-pie" premise, wherein a limited amount of personal power is available to be allo-cated, in various-sized slices, among all the family members. From this perspective, as maturing children seek larger pieces of the fam-ily's power-pie, parents feel as if their personal slices are being nibbled away to nothing.

I believe this is the major reason some parents subtly or openly compete with their growing children, especially their same-sex chil-dren. Many fathers continually need to reaffirm their "king of the mountain" positions as possessors of the largest slices of the family's power-pie. Typically, such fathers convene this competition in arenas that supply *their* greatest sense of personal power, for example those involving physical strength, athletic prowess, intellectual ability, pro-fessional success and the like. In a feminine variation on this theme, mothers may compete just as ferociously to maintain superior status over their daughters on family battlefields of sexual attractiveness, social adeptness and personal competence.

Sadly, as a result of their own shame-based feelings of inadequacy, these fathers and mothers don't feel big and powerful unless they keep their sons and daughters small and powerless. If you recognize any of these child-releasing resistances in yourself, you may be eager to turn a corner with me as we consider some strategies for learning to let go without strings attached.

Practical Strategies for Giving Wings

1. We must begin by honestly evaluating our beliefs and attitudes about releasing our children. Figure 13-1 displays contrasting beliefs that we live out in our parenting as we meet our children's developmental steps with either shame-strings or grace-wings.

Contrasting Approaches to Releasing Our Children

Grace-Full Attitude (Wings)	Shame-Full Attitudes (Strings)
Underlying Belief: Parents are supposed to give their children unconditional love and wise guidance to help them grow up into gradually increasing self-reliance and sense of responsibility (ideally, under the lordship of Jesus Christ).	*Underlying Belief:* Children are supposed to give their parents unconditional love and always stay feeling "grown down" and totally responsible for their parents' happiness so the parents can avoid feeling lonely/abandoned and also avoid taking personal responsibility for their own lives.
Background Focus: I am always in a process of releasing my children by gradually transferring total responsibility for my children from me to them. I reward each of their "baby steps" on the path to separation and individuation.	*Background Focus:* I'm always keeping my children as parent-focused as I can by making them feel totally responsible for me and/or by continuing to take total responsibility for them. I punish each "baby step" toward individuation.
Immediate Focus: I do my present parenting tasks as well as possible and also try to anticipate and prepare myself and my children for upcoming developmental changes.	*Immediate Focus:* I meet my present, personal needs as much as possible by keeping my children dependent on me so that I can feel loved and needed and/or powerful.
Example of "Gracing": When my teen consistently demonstrates trustworthiness, I grant his/her request to spend spring break at the beach with a close friend and his/her family.	*Example of "Shaming":* When my teen asks to spend spring break with a close friend and his/her family, I tell my child he/she is too young for that and I imply he/she is selfish for wanting to "abandon" me.

Figure 13-1.

We will always live what we believe. This means that if I believe my children exist now and always to satisfy my need for unconditional love or superior power, my parenting will be strikingly different from that of adults who believe that parents should lovingly anticipate and meet their children's changing needs for the ultimate purpose of helping them develop lives of their own that glorify their Creator.

2. After we have honestly evaluated our beliefs about releasing our children, we need to examine our current releasing styles. Review figure 13-1 to see whether your current attitudes and actions fall more into the grace-full or the shame-full category. We may be able to recognize our styles more easily when our children are older, but we will behaviorally express our underlying beliefs even when they are babies.

Whether our children are two, ten or twenty, wise parents respect their attempts to gain control of and take responsibility for their own lives. Obviously we don't allow toddlers to make the same kinds of decisions we let teens make. But if we can accept a toddler's blatant push for personal mastery without entangling him or her in shame-strings, we will be better prepared for our teens' more sophisticated tactics.

3. We need to actively and prayerfully seek and begin using healthier, more biblical methods of releasing our children. We can ask our most shame-free friends how they negotiate the tightrope between hurrying up and holding back their children. And we can read good books on this topic. To get you started, here are a few letting-go-with-wings ideas for parents of young children, adolescents and adults.

Wings for Young Children

1. Celebrate milestones in your children's development. When we recognize and rejoice in our children's growth steps, they get the message that we love them as they are *and* as they change. Devel-

opmental milestones include a first tooth, first steps, first day of school, and so on.

2. Anticipate and prepare for children's upcoming developmental changes. We won't be blindsided by a child's strange new behavior if we know what's around the developmental corner. And when our children are old enough, we need to discuss imminent changes with them to prepare them as much as possible for the new challenges introduced at each growth step. For example, it is critically important to educate our prepubescent children about the physical and emotional changes soon to convulse their lives.

3. As much as possible, refuse to do for your children what they can do for themselves. Let them organize their activities, occupy themselves and solve social and academic problems, for the most part, on their own. This is how our children learn to think, persevere and be resourceful, and these are indispensable traits in responsible adults.

4. Begin allowing children to experience the consequences of their choices (without endangering their health or lives, of course). We wouldn't allow a toddler to experience the consequences of choosing to play in the street. But we prepare our children for adult realities and responsibilities when (rather than pull a rescue) we allow them to miss lunch and class assignment deadlines when they forget their book bags. These uncomfortable lessons may help them avoid far more painful choices and consequences in adolescence and beyond.

Wings for Adolescents

1. Continue to celebrate developmental milestones in your teens. In the last chapter, I described the room redecoration "releasing ritual" we used to formally mark our children's entrances into their teens. At the time, I didn't think of it as a releasing ritual. It was just sort of a Gentile *bar mitzvah!* A first job, a first date, a new driver's license are all significant adolescent milestones to celebrate.

2. Purposefully plan "empowering opportunities" for your teens. If we sincerely seek more respectful and biblical parenting patterns

for letting go of our children, we must learn to value the concept of *empowering.* Jesus used power not to control and enslave but to serve and to save.[1] He used it "to lift the fallen, forgive the guilty, to encourage responsibility and maturity in the weak and to empower the powerless."[2]

Parental empowering is the developmentally paced process of instilling confidence and building up children by recognizing their strengths and by affirming their abilities to learn, to grow and to become all God created them to be. From a biblical perspective, empowering does *not* mean children gain power at the expense of parents' losses of power. When Jesus told the disciples that they soon would *receive* power (Acts 1:8), he was in no danger of *losing* any. The wing-clipping, limited "power-pie" view is not God's idea.

Because of differences in resources and status, parents have power over their children that can attach strings or create wings—bind or empower. It is extremely unlikely that you or I will *become* empowering until we *receive* empowering through the unconditional, redeeming love of God. But when we do, this grace-based, life-transforming relationship with our perfect heavenly Parent can become the primary source of our unconditional love and personal significance. Then we will be secure and free enough to empower our children by loving them to security and freeing them to become empowerers. In so doing, we change the intergenerational cycle of shame-stringing that binds and confines children of all ages into less than they could be.

Ideally, we begin gently fashioning empowering wings for our children from birth. But when they reach adolescence, we must shift this process into high gear by purposefully designing confidence-building, ability-stretching opportunities. We can give teens more "soaring" freedom in social activities, assign them more household responsibilities and plan dozens of other ways to empower them as we acknowledge their increasing maturity.

3. Explicitly authorize your adolescent's process of "individuation."

In a sense, each of us defines ourselves as we sift values, tastes and opinions to determine which belong to our parents or peers and which are part of what truly defines us as a unique individual. Ideally, we master much of this self-defining task in adolescence. But in families headed by insecure, impaired parents, teens rarely get to do that. Some of us still wear the *disloyal-child* label because we tried. Others of us still haven't tried. (This may be why we often feel confused when someone asks us what we like, or even who we are.)

In effect, authorizing individuation provides the wind beneath the wings we have been fashioning for our children. This authorizing enterprise means openly discussing inevitable, yet annoying, parent-teen tussles. Sometimes it means adapting to new names. I remember when our *David* became *Dave.* We also allow teens to flex their emerging individuality when we tolerate hairstyles and fashions deemed outrageous by our standards. (Of course, our standards are deemed archaic by our teens!) No, I don't mean we let them head for high school nearly nude. But half-shaved heads grow out and triple-pierced ears are seldom fatal—even in males.

When we allow our teens to stage safe, small rebellions like these, they usually find it unnecessary to wage World War 3 for a sense of separateness. In effect, they are less apt to make it *rough* on the family when we explicitly authorize the individuation tasks that *smooth* their paths into healthy adult interdependence.

But what if we didn't understand any of this until after our children were grown? It's still not too late to learn to give wings.

Wings for Adult Children

1. If you have hindered and shame-strung your adult children in their healthy, human drives for separateness, admit it to them. I didn't say *confess* it because I don't believe it is a sin to be ignorant of what we've never been taught. But certainly we can express sincere regret that we did not know sooner what we are learning now. An old Dutch proverb says it this way: *"Too soon old, too late smart!"*

2. Aim for a more mutually respectful and reciprocal relationship with your adult children. In substantially shame-free relationships, both parties have something to give and both are able to receive. In contrast, most shame-based relationships between adults are unbalanced and custodial—one adult is in charge and takes care of the other. Relating custodially to our children is appropriate and realistic when they are young. It is inappropriate and disrespectful when they are adults.

3. Make new choices that move the relationships with your adult children toward greater equality. In effect, you and I need to create a more level playing field where we and our adult children can look each other in the eye as equals.[3] If we make this a serious goal, we probably will need to make serious changes in our choices, both as our parents' adult children *and* as our adult children's parents. Here are some examples:

☐ If we get goodies by letting *our* parents "retain custody" of *us,* we need to be willing to give them up. These goodies could be material, such as present financial support or a promised inheritance, or emotional, such as parental approval awarded for parental control. Our adult children are apt to be pretty unconvinced that we value reciprocal adult relationships if they see us consistently allowing our parents to rescue and/or control us.

☐ We must allow our adult children to give as well as to receive. For example, if we always handle the entire bill when we dine out with our grown children, how about letting them pay for a change? At least they can leave the tip.

☐ We need to retire from our roles as "everything experts." In other words, stop giving your adult children unsolicited advice as if you were the leading expert in the world on every subject in the world. You're not. Neither am I, but I sometimes forget that.

Recently Garth and I drove to Atlanta to see our son and daughter-in-law and our three-month-old granddaughter. Dabney was thriving with her folks' loving care and her mommy's commitment to breast-feed. But since the pediatrician told Dru that the baby needed to get accustomed to an occasional bottle, she had dutifully introduced one several times a week. Based on Dabney's high-decibel response, she was *not* thrilled.

One afternoon, with Dru near tears from trying to give her wailing daughter a bottle, I leaped in to play "baby-feeding expert." I dispensed several priceless gems of wisdom which proved to be more confusing than comforting at that high-stress moment. Then, in a heroically healthy boundary-setting move, Dave kindly but firmly told me that he and Dru needed to decide when to give Dabney a bottle and I was not being helpful.

I immediately apologized to Dru and Dave, as Garth tossed me one of those eye-rolling looks that say, "And *she* writes books about dysfunctional families!" After the bottle-feeding crisis subsided, I congratulated Dave for saying what he did as well as for when and how he said it. As I've reflected on that afternoon, my joy that Dave felt free to "speak the truth in love" to his well-meaning but meddling mother has substantially offset my guilt about butting in with unsolicited advice.

If your adult children are not as comfortable setting boundaries as Dave is, you may need to give them permission *repeatedly* to resist your "everything expert" role. And if you really want to jolt your grown kids, refuse to give them even *solicited* advice! For a liberating change, try saying something like, "I'd like to hear your ideas on that," or, "I think maybe I give you too much advice. Do what you think is best."

☐ We need to retire from our roles as "pain buffers" and "safety nets." You've probably heard of buffered aspirin; well, we can create "buffered children" when, out of earnest but unwise love, we cushion them from the consequences of their irresponsible choices. In other words, we may function as buffers between the kids who desperately need to change and the pain God might use to begin changing them.

And even when our adult children are reasonably responsible, we may be woven into their lives and strung across their struggles like human safety nets. We are the "ace in the hole," their ever-present back door of escape when times get tough. It seems so cruel to think about standing back and watching our children, and perhaps our grandchildren, face genuine difficulties—especially when we have the resources to rescue them.

The problem is that we only get to play "big, strong, wonderful rescuer" by making our adult children play "small, weak, pathetic victim." That's not exactly empowering them! But what if adult children keep *volunteering* for the "weak one" role? (And of course they will, if we have taught them "well.")

☐ As a last resort, we need to "play dead." I agree this sounds terrible, but it can be terribly effective. Preparing our children to soar in healthy interdependence is a process, not an event. Our job is to gently, firmly nudge our children along in this process by encouraging them to truthfully confront reality at each step. When our adult children insist on clinging to immature overdependence, we might have to jump-start their stalled maturing process by confronting them with this inescapable, onrushing truth: they will not always have us around to kiss the "boo-boos" of life and make them all better. With this reality in view, we love most wisely by pointing our adult children to the empowering, ever-living Christ who can meet all the needs of life.

But what if our children don't care about Christ or his provisions?

Releasing Our Prodigals
Even sincerely devoted Christians like Ruth and Billy Graham know the pain of having prodigal children.[4] And if we have not even *attempted,* however imperfectly, to live Christian values before our children, we can experience lacerating guilt if they wander into pagan pigpens.

At such times we may be tempted to either completely reject or continually rescue our prodigals. Neither extreme triggers homecomings. *We must lovingly detach from our prodigal children.* "Loving detachment" means cutting the strings of attempted control and accepting our powerlessness to change another person, even when that person is our self-destructive adult child whom we deeply love.

Chances are it's too late to control them with entreaties of love or threats of wrath—ours or God's. This is the time to stop talking to our children about God and to start talking to God about our children. No pigpen is beyond the reach of God's grace. And in the final analysis, we must do with our prodigals what we need to do with all our children—cut the strings and release them to the Father's fierce and faithful love.

Personal Reflection

Answer the following questions to assess your "releasing readiness."

1. Do you think it's a sin for adult children to disobey their parents' wishes?

2. Do you lack a sense of personal identity and worth apart from your children?

3. Do you remind your children how much they "owe you" with recitations about risking your health to give them birth or ruining your happiness to give them a better home and education than you had?

4. Do you see the end of "custodial parenting" as the beginning of loneliness?

5. Do you keep trying to gently control your grown children's choices? (For their own good, of course.)

6. Do you and your spouse have a difficult time finding anything to talk about except your children and their activities?

7. Do you frequently give your adult children substantial sums of money to help them buy things they deeply desire? (Only to be kind, of course.)

8. Do your adult children ask your advice about nearly every decision they must make?

If you answered yes to more than one question, you probably need to reevaluate your beliefs about parent-child relationships. You may also need to refocus your attention and priorities from your children to your relationships with God, yourself and your spouse or friends.

Looking Ahead

What's left of parenting after letting go of our children? As most of us know *so* well, a parent's power to influence lingers long past a child's departure from home—for better or for worse.

In the next chapter we'll find hope and help for using our influence to turn our parenting "worse" into something "better."

14
Life-Giving
Legacies

Y ou may have begun this book as a confused, discouraged parent desperately wanting to improve your children's behavior. Now here you are starting the last chapter, perhaps more confused and discouraged about a wider range of both parenting and personal issues. You may be desiring even *more* desperately to change your children. But now you have to confront my assertion that you can't really do that, although you *do* need to change yourself. Said differently, you may feel as if you're right where you started—only *more* so!

Believe me, I know the feeling. And so does every person who earnestly pursues the freedom and wholeness which truth brings. This sense of "more-so," of issues being more problem-laden and painful than we originally knew, reflects the old maxim that "truth makes us free but usually it first makes us miserable."

We Can't Go Back

If this describes your situation right now, I have some bad news: *we can't go back.* Once we've begun to recognize the truth about how we were parented and how we've parented our children, we can't go back to the familiar misery of that's-just-how-my-family-is, business-as-usual living. Oh, we may try to go back by refusing to change our living and our parenting. But we can't go back completely to the familiar, uninformed misery we formerly "enjoyed."

I also have some *good* news: *we can't go back.* We see the lies of shame more clearly now. We understand more about why we hurt and about why, in our pain, we hurt our children and others. As we recognize the ways we've chosen to cope with our personal pain, we can fully "own" those choices and then make healthier new ones. Laying aside our sincere and tear-stained "if-onlys" is one of these healthier new choices.

Starting Over Again

"Could everything be done twice everything would be done better," says an old proverb.[1] That's so true of our parenting, isn't it? I've already admitted wrestling repeatedly with the walloping "if-onlys" when I consider *my* parenting. Here's how another parent expressed *her* if-onlys:

> If only I could have them as babies again. I'd write detailed and wondrous descriptions in their baby books. I'd hold them closer and longer. I'd read to them more. I'd play with them more. If only they were toddlers again. I'd take them for walks. I'd have spontaneous winter picnics on the living room floor. I'd take more pictures of them. I'd put the ones I took into albums. *If only I could start over again.*[2]

I have wonderful news for this mom and all the rest of us painfully imperfect moms and dads racked with regrets. We can start over again—and again and again!

No, we can't rewrite history and go back to the beginning of our parenting paths. But we can begin anew right where we are. And if we do, we'll meet some pretty illustrious predecessors in this starting-over process.

The God of Second Times

I am the only person I know whose favorite Bible verse is Jonah 3:1, which says: "Then the word of the LORD came to Jonah a second time."

I love that verse! It tells me that God is just exactly the kind of God I desperately need, because he is a God of "second times." I don't know about you. But, believe me, I've needed an awful lot of second and twenty-second and two hundred twenty-second times in my life. Like Jonah, I spent a brief but intensely miserable time running from God's revealed will. I reel in horror contemplating where I would be now if God hadn't brought me his Word a *second* time.

This precious Old Testament verse dimly illumines the truth and grace which Jesus incarnated in blinding, incandescent perfection. (See Jn 1:14.) "The word of the Lord" is God's truth. The fact that he gave it to his rebellious, reluctant prophet "a second time" reveals God's grace. Perfect people would get everything right the first time, I suppose. Sin-broken people like Jonah and me need "second times." I'm inexpressibly grateful that new beginnings are part of God's plan!

New Beginnings

You may be thinking that all this starting-over stuff is fine for Bible characters and for people who write books, but it's not for you. Maybe you believe you've ruined your life and your children by behavior that barricades the path to new beginnings. It's true that we profoundly wound our children with our sinful behaviors. And it's also true that we have to do more than try to read, talk, cry and pray our way out of the personal and parenting problems we have behaved our way into. We must change our behavior, and this means changing our choices. And that means we need help.

Shame says we should be perfect and problem-free or at least look that way. Shame excludes the possibility of asking for help. But to begin anew as increasingly shame-free people and parents we need help to separate the lies that have bound us from the life-liberating truths we must learn to believe and begin to live.

When we choose to begin living in the light of God's truth, we and our children will never be the same, for there is one choice that is not ours. *We cannot choose to remain unchanged by truth.* Only we ourselves can determine whether our responses to the truths we've explored will be for better or worse. "Worse" is continuing to contribute to our children's bondage to lies and shame just as our parents contributed to ours. "Better" is contributing to our children's freedom by choosing truth-based, God-honoring new beginnings.

How do we recognize these new beginnings? What do they look like? They can look something like one Christian wife and mother I'll call Crissta. Raised by an alcoholic, promiscuous father and a passively controlling mother, at seventeen Crissta married an angry and alcoholic young man named Joe. The first of their three children came when neither Crissta nor Joe had the emotional energy or living skills to be a consistently adequate parent.

A coworker's appealingly different Christian lifestyle interested Joe in "this Jesus guy" who was supposed to be able to give a meaningful new life to sinful, hopeless people if they asked him. Joe asked, and Jesus gave. After seeing significant changes in her newly sober husband, Crissta asked Jesus into her life too. Eventually they found a Christ-centered and nurturing church family, where both got counseling to unload the shame-stuffed baggage they had dragged into their adult lives.

At my request, Crissta wrote about her parenting regrets and her personal reflections on the starting-over process in the following letter to her twelve-year-old daughter.

Dear _____,

Now that I have _____ [two-year-old] and _____
[seven-month-old], I think a lot about what kind of a parent I was
when you were little. I think about all that you went through and
what kind of a home you had as a small child.

As I learn about the ways my dysfunctional family hurt me as
a child, I find myself looking at you and wondering. I feel bad
about the way I parented you then and sometimes even now
when I blow it.

The more my eyes are opened about the unhealthy ways I relate
to others, the more I see that "I've taught you everything I know."
Thankfully, the Lord has opened my eyes while there is still time.
I am becoming healthy.

As I learn to set boundaries, calmly relate and be honest, I see
you are learning as well. As the Lord changes me he changes my
whole family.

Now I don't feel so driven to volunteer myself to death trying
to "be somebody." I don't feel that rage that drove me to scream
so often. (I always hated that as a child.) Now I can be emotionally
available.

I thank God for that. As I continue to slow down and grow in
the Lord, I feel more and more hopeful. I am finally breaking free
of my compulsions and taking better care of myself and you.

The best reward is the encouragement I get from you. I love
you!

                                                                    Mom

If you could talk to Crissta, she would tell you that she still needs
lots of "second times" because—just like all of us—she isn't a perfect
mom. But she surely is a healthier, more shame-free mom. And she
is living the reality of Christ's power to change those who seek new
beginnings.

Like Jonah, Crissta and me, you too can start over again. That's a promise from the God who graciously designed "second times." And when our children see us choosing God's truth after existing so long in bondage to shame's lies, they learn that they too can experience the Lord's redeeming love and gracious "second times."

Through Locked Doors

Of course we have no guarantee that our children will always choose the life-giving truths of God that we have begun to choose. In fact, your children may have locked you out of their lives as a result of some of your earlier, deeply hurtful choices. If this is the case, I have some more good news: Jesus can go through locked doors!

Open your Bible to the twentieth chapter of John's Gospel and let the verses stimulate your mind's eye. Can you see that little group of terrified disciples huddled together in secret behind bolted doors? Their hopes stirred with news of Jesus' empty tomb, but their hearts were still full of grief and doubt.

Then it happened! Right through the locked door came Jesus! Can't you imagine the bug-eyed, incredulous looks on the disciples' faces? No wonder Jesus' first words to them were, "Peace be with you."

Jesus can go where we're barred. Jesus can touch those who shrink from our wounding words and hands. Locked doors didn't deter Jesus when he was on earth in flesh, and they don't stop him now.

If we have lived and parented by shame-based lies, we have sown seeds of destruction. And for some of us it's too late to pray for just a crop failure! We need the One who brings life out of death.

No ordinary, reasonable, run-of-the-mill hope will get us through the killing fields of our parenting memories. We need unreasonable, you've-got-to-be-out-of-your-mind, empty-tomb hope. Only Jesus can supply that. Pour out all your regret and despair to him. Dump it all at his feet. Receive his forgiveness and peace. And trust him to love open the hearts that are locked to you. Even when our children and others we love won't receive us, they may yet receive Christ.

Plutarch said, "My family history begins with me." In a sense this is semantic sleight-of-hand, considering our ancestors' influences on our parents and on us. Yet it is true in another, more hopeful sense. For regardless of what has gone before, you and I have the opportunity to profoundly alter what comes after us.

Generations from now, I want my grandchild and her grandchildren's grandchildren to look back and see that although I repeatedly failed, by the grace of God who loved me and gave himself for me, I loved God and began anew to live in his truth. And that made all the difference.

Come join me in building and bequeathing life-giving legacies as we follow Jesus and receive his tomb-emptying power for our shame-free parenting.

Appendix A

Physical Indicators of Sexual Abuse[1]
1. Pain or itching in genital area
2. Difficulty in walking or sitting
3. Vaginal discharge
4. Bruises or bleeding in external genitalia, vaginal or anal regions
5. Venereal disease, especially in children
6. Swollen or red cervix, vulva or perineum
7. Pregnancy when a child refuses to reveal any information about the father or there is a complete denial of pregnancy by the child or her parents
8. Torn, stained or bloody underclothing
9. Unusual and offensive odors

Behavioral Indicators of Sexual Abuse in Infants and Preschoolers
1. Being uncomfortable around previously trusted persons
2. Sexualized behavior (excessive masturbation, sexually inserting objects, explicit sex play with other children)
3. Fear of rest rooms, showers or baths (common locations of abuse)
4. Fear of being alone with men or boys
5. Nightmares on a regular basis or about the same person
6. Abrupt personality changes
7. Uncharacteristic hyperactivity
8. Moodiness, excessive crying
9. Aggressive or violent behavior toward other children
10. Difficulty in sleeping or relaxing

11. Clinging behavior which may take the form of separation anxiety

12. Passive or withdrawn behavior

Behavioral Indicators of Sexual Abuse in Elementary-School-Aged Children

1. Being uncomfortable around previously trusted persons

2. Specific knowledge of sexual facts and terminology beyond developmental stage

3. Sexual behavior (excessive masturbation, sexual acting out with other children on a regular basis, seductive toward peers and adults)

4. Wearing multiple layers of clothing, especially to bed

5. "Parentified" behavior (pseudo-mature, acts like a small parent)

6. Fear of being alone with men or boys

7. Fear of rest rooms, showers or baths

8. Constant, unexplained anxiety, tension or fear

9. Frequent tardiness or absence from school, especially if male caretaker writes excuses

10. Attempts to make herself ugly or undesirable (poor personal hygiene, weight problems)

11. Abrupt personality changes

12. Tendency to seek out or totally avoid adults

Behavioral Indicators of Sexual Abuse in Adolescents

1. Sexualized behavior (promiscuity, prostitution, sexual abuse of younger children)

2. Running away, especially in a child not normally a behavior problem

3. Drug and alcohol abuse

4. Suicidal gestures or attempts

5. Self-mutilation

6. Extreme hostility toward a parent or caretaker

7. Defiance or compliance to an extreme

Behavioral Indicators of Sexual Abuse in Adults

1. Sexual difficulties (usually regarding intimacy issues)

2. Distrust of the opposite sex

3. Inappropriate choice of partners (chooses a dependent partner she can mother or one who abuses her or her children physically or sexually)

4. Progressive breakdown of communication and eventual emotional detachment from children

5. Multiple marriages

6. Extreme dependence upon or anger toward a parent

7. Sexual promiscuity (or alternating between periods of preoccupation with and revulsion by sexual activity)

8. Drug or alcohol abuse

9. Extremely low self-esteem

10. Nightmares or flashbacks

11. Continual victimization (seemingly unable to assert or protect herself)

12. Seeing own worth only in terms of sexuality

13. Eating disorders (usually obesity)

14. Self-punishing behaviors
15. Homosexual orientation[2]
16. Body shame (extreme self-consciousness)

In addition to these behavioral indicators, listed by David Peters, I think the following are also significant when they appear within a cluster of other indicators in adults.

1. Sleep disturbances, such as fear of the dark or of sleeping alone, nightmares of pursuit

2. Throat or breathing problems, such as frequent, stress-related sore throats, swallowing and gagging sensitivity; suffocating feelings (including repugnance to water on face when bathing or swimming). Note: these throat/breathing/gagging symptoms, when taken together with a cluster of other indicators, suggest the possibility of oral rape

3. Alienation from the body—not feeling "at home" in one's own body; insensitivity to signals from own body; poor body care or distorted body image

4. Unusual clothing habits, such as preference for baggy, body-concealing clothes, wearing layers of clothing even in summer; sleeping fully or heavily clothed (for example, in sweats); resistance to removing clothing when bathing or swimming

5. Touch aversion—excessive dislike and/or fear of being touched (especially without warning)

6. Repressed tears or screams—feeling desire or need to scream or sob; hearing a child scream or sob *inside* head

7. Trance, depersonalization, dissociation, that is, disconnecting from present reality, going numb or into internal "safe place" in a stressful situation associated with particular emotions such as anger, memories or situations, such as intercourse

Appendix B

Shame-Based vs. Grace-Based Church Families

Shame-full Church Family

Rooted in shame-based religionism; keeping human-made rules in order to be "right."

God is experienced as a demanding Shepherd who drives his sheep.

I am expected to be totally (or almost totally) transformed the moment I trust Christ.

Since I should be totally transformed (perfect) I am a different-and-less-than Christian because I'm not perfect.

Members with obvious problems are an embarrassment to the church. Since real Christians have no serious problems, no provisions have been made to help.

Small-group Bible studies are dangerous places because someone might get close enough to see behind my mask of perfection and know I have problems.

Emphasis is on looking religious by wearing the right clothes and carrying the right translation of the Bible.

Emphasis is on performance.

Emphasis is on revealing and rebuking sinners.

Attendance at church activities is used as the main indicator of a person's true spirituality.

Grace-full Church Family

Rooted in grace-based relationship; trusting in Christ's death and resurrection in order to be "right."

God is experienced as an understanding Shepherd who leads his sheep.

I am expected to keep on being transformed by having my mind renewed as long as I live.

Since I am in a lifelong process of being transformed to be like Jesus, my imperfections don't surprise me, church members or God.

Members with obvious problems are expected since the past and present effects of sin in Christians' lives can cause serious problems. There are programs in place to provide appropriate help.

Small-group Bible studies are safe places to practice being maskless and be with others who do the same. It's great to go where I don't have to hide my problems.

Emphasis is on developing a deeper relationship of love and trusting obedience with Jesus Christ.

Emphasis is on worshiping God.

Emphasis is on restoring repentant sinners.

Acknowledgment that true spirituality is reflected in total lifestyle and known only to God.

Appendix C

Resources

Note: After related chapters in my book *Released from Shame* (Downers Grove, Ill.: InterVarsity Press, 1990) are cited, additional books are listed alphabetically. All are written from a clearly Christian perspective except those preceded by an open square symbol: ☐.

FOR CHAPTERS 1—3
Reading chapters 1—7 of *Released from Shame* will enrich your understanding of topics covered in these chapters.

FOR CHAPTER 4 Choosing Grace: Releasing
Released from Shame, chapter 12.

Augsburger, David. *Freedom of Forgiveness.* Chicago: Moody Press, 1986. This forgiveness classic motivates and guides readers to forgive "as Christ would."

Guest, Joan Lloyd. *Forgiving Your Parents: How Adult Children Can Heal Past Hurts.* Downers Grove, Ill.: InterVarsity Press, 1988. Page for page, this little booklet is the best buy available to help us do what the title says.

Stanley, Charles. *Forgiveness.* Nashville: Oliver Nelson, 1989. This well-known pastor gives biblical and practical guidelines for forgiving.

Walters, Richard. *Forgive and Be Free.* Grand Rapids, Mich.: Zondervan, 1983. This small book is loaded with real-life examples of forgiving—the process and the benefits. Walters even includes a "Forgiveness Contract" among his useful suggestions.

FOR CHAPTER 5 We Can Learn What We Don't Know
Balswick, Jack, and Judith Balswick. *The Family.* Grand Rapids, Mich.: Baker Book House, 1989. This book is a comprehensive, clearly biblical treasure house of wisdom about families and parenting.

Curran, Dolores. *Traits of a Healthy Family.* New York: Ballantine Books/Epiphany, 1983. This is must reading for those of us who have only a vague idea of what healthy families look like.

☐ Clarke, Jean Illsley. *Self-Esteem: A Family Affair.* New York: Harper & Row, 1978. This book is filled with great ideas about giving affirming messages and avoiding "don't be" messages to our children, plus lots of other good stuff.

☐ Clarke, Jean Illsley, and Connie Dawson. *Growing Up Again: Parenting Ourselves and Our Children.* Center City, Minn.: Hazelden, 1989. Clarke, with coauthor Dawson, gives us another gem of parenting wisdom with information about developmental stages and ideas about how to ask for change without attacking a child's worth, plus much more.

Fryling, Alice, and Robert Fryling. *A Handbook for Parents.* Downers Grove, Ill.: Inter-Varsity Press, 1991. This is a small gem of parenting wisdom.

☐ Rolfe, Randy Colton. *Adult Children Raising Children.* Deerfield Beach, Fla.: 1989. Rolfe provides an abundance of general insight and practical ideas to help the parents described in her title.

Smalley, Gary, and John Trent. *The Blessing.* Nashville: Thomas Nelson, 1986. The authors tell us how to recognize the effects of receiving or not receiving "The Blessing" in our own lives. We also receive directions for giving The Blessing to our children and spouses.

Stanley, Charles. *How to Keep Your Kids on Your Team.* Nashville: Thomas Nelson, 1986. A biblical action plan for caring parents.

FOR CHAPTER 6 We Can Learn and Teach About God
Released from Shame, chapter 11.

Chapin, Alice. *Building Your Child's Faith.* Nashville: Thomas Nelson, 1990. Chapin offers creative ideas and practical suggestions for developing our children's "basic ingredients" of faith: worship, Bible reading, Scripture memorization and prayer.

Hromas, Robert. *52 Simple Ways to Teach Your Child to Pray.* Nashville: Thomas Nelson, 1991. The title says it all.

Morgenthaler, Shirley K. *Right from the Start: A New Parent's Guide to Child Faith Development.* St. Louis: Concordia, 1989. I wish I had been able to read this excellent book when my children were young.

Spackman, Carl K. *Parents Passing On the Faith.* Wheaton, Ill.: Victor Books, 1989. A pastor gives ideas to help parents equip children to cope with life in an evil world.

Temple, Todd. *52 Simple Ways to Teach Your Child About God.* Nashville: Thomas Nelson, 1991. The title says it all.

FOR CHAPTER 7 We Can Learn to Really Love Our Children
Released from Shame, chapter 8.

Arteburn, Stephen, and Carl Dreizler. *52 Simple Ways to Tell Your Child "I Love You."* Nashville: Thomas Nelson, 1991. The title says it all.

Beers, Gilbert V. *Best Friends for Life: Building Lifelong Relationships with Your Children.* Eugene, Ore.: Harvest House, 1988. This book has lots of good ideas for doing what the title suggests.

Brawner, Jim, with Duncan Jaenicke. *Connections: Using Personality Types to Draw Parents and Kids Closer.* Chicago: Moody Press, 1991. This Christian educator helps parents understand and value their children's individuality.

Campbell, Ross. *How to Really Love Your Child.* Wheaton, Ill.: Victor Books, 1977. This excellent book has become a parenting classic—and rightly so.

Smalley, Gary, and John Trent. *The Gift of Honor.* Nashville: Thomas Nelson, 1987.

Another excellent book from authors who help us understand the role of honor in our lives and in the lives of those we love.

FOR CHAPTER 8 We Can Learn to Have Realistic Expectations
Released from Shame, chapter 8.

Dargatz, Jan. *52 Simple Ways to Build Your Child's Self-Esteem and Confidence.* Nashville: Thomas Nelson, 1991. The title says it all.

Hart, Archibald. *Stress and Your Child.* Dallas: Word Books, 1991. Because children are exposed to high levels of stress today, Hart tells parents how to recognize stress and teach children good coping habits.

Lehman, Kevin. *Getting the Best Out of Your Kids.* Eugene, Ore.: Harvest House, 1991. With humor and practical strategies, Lehman tells parents how to help a child overcome discouragement, how to be our children's best teacher and much more.

McDowell, Josh, and Dick Day. *How to Be a Hero to Your Kids.* Dallas: Word Books, 1991. The authors show parents concrete steps for becoming good role models for our kids.

FOR CHAPTER 9 We Can Learn to Communicate with Talk and Touch
□ Helmstetter, Shad. *Predictive Parenting: What to Say When You Talk to Your Kids.* New York: Pocket Books, 1989. The author provides lots of very practical ideas for preventing problems before they occur.

Jenkins, Jerry. *Twelve Things I Want My Kids to Remember.* Chicago: Moody Press, 1992. This dad tells parents how to effectively communicate "the essentials."

Pelfrey, Wanda B. *Making the Most of Your Child's Teachable Moments.* Chicago: Moody Press, 1988. This book is filled with simple suggestions for using everyday events to teach children about God and life.

Smalley, Gary. *The Key to Your Child's Heart.* Dallas: Word Books, 1987. Smalley helps parents tenderly open their children's hearts instead of wounding them.

Wright, H. Norman. *The Power of a Parent's Words.* Ventura, Calif.: Regal Books, 1991. Parents get persuasive reasons and practical resources for improving communication with their children.

FOR CHAPTER 10 We Can Learn to Feel Good About Feelings
Released from Shame, chapter 9.

Oliver, Gary J., and H. Norman Wright. *When Anger Hits Home.* Chicago: Moody Press, 1992. This helpful book contains specific steps to constructively harness anger's power.

FOR CHAPTER 11 We Can Learn to Like Limits
Released from Shame, chapter 10.

Anson, Elva. *How to Get Kids to Help at Home.* Chicago: Moody Press, 1990. Children who help at home learn skills and principles to help them become capable and independent.

Backus, William, and Candace Backus. *Empowering Parents.* Minneapolis: Bethany House, 1992. The authors give parents ten "long-term values" to help children become responsible and confident adults.

Hancock, Maxine, and Karen Mains. *Child Sexual Abuse: A Hope for Healing.* Wheaton,

Ill.: Shaw, 1987. These authors have studied and counseled adults scarred by child sexual abuse. They offer sensitive, specific strategies for understanding and healing such abuse.

Peters, David. *A Betrayal of Innocence: What Everyone Should Know About Child Sexual Abuse.* Dallas: Word Books, 1986. This is a classic among Christian books on the topic.

☐ Rosemond, John. *Parent Power!* Kansas City, Mo.: Andrews/McMeel, 1991. This family counselor gives many practical suggestions for empowering parents.

Sanford, Doris. *I Can Say No: A Child's Book About Drug Abuse.* Portland, Ore.: Multnomah Press, 1990. This author, in collaboration with a gifted illustrator, has a marvelous series of beautiful books about painful childhood issues, all written on a child's level.

———. *I Can't Talk About It: A Child's Book About Sexual Abuse.* Portland, Ore.: Multnomah Press, 1989.

———. *Don't Make Me Go Back, Mommy: A Child's Book About Satanic Ritual Abuse.* Portland, Ore.: Multnomah Press, 1990.

FOR CHAPTER 12 We Can Learn to Have Fun (If We Work at It!)

Dargatz, Jan. *52 Simple Ways to Make Christmas Special.* Nashville: Thomas Nelson, 1991. The title says it all.

Dreizler, Carl. *52 Simple Ways to Have Fun with Your Child.* Nashville: Thomas Nelson, 1991. The title says it all.

Hadidian, Allen, Connie Hadidian, Will Wilson, and Lindy Wilson. *Creative Family Times.* Chicago: Moody Press, 1990. The authors give specific ideas for planning fun and purposeful activities.

FOR CHAPTER 13 We Can Learn to Give Wings Not Strings

Baucom, John. *Bonding and Breaking Free.* Grand Rapids, Mich.: Zondervan, 1988. This book helps parents both nurture and clearly empower their children.

Campbell, Ross. *How to Really Love Your Teenager.* Wheaton, Ill.: Victor Books, 1982. Another Campbell classic full of practical, biblical ideas for parenting teens.

Coleman, William. *How to Go Home Without Feeling like a Child.* Dallas: Word Books, 1991. Practical advice for creating a "level playing field" for parents and their grown children.

Kuykendall, Carol. *Learning to Let Go.* Grand Rapids, Mich.: Zondervan, 1985. Here's a helpful resource for learning how to give wings instead of strings.

☐ Pockat, Debra. *How to Detach with Love: A Parent's Guide to Detachment.* Chicago: Parkside, 1989. This is a useful resource to help parents lovingly detach from chemically dependent teens and adult children. To order call 1-800-221-6364; in Illinois call 312-698-8550.

White, John. *Parents in Pain.* Downers Grove, Ill.: InterVarsity Press, 1979. A classic of encouragement for parents agonizing over their children.

FOR CHAPTER 14 Life-Giving Legacies

Released from Shame, chapter 13.

Backus, William, and Candace Backus. *What Did I Do Wrong? What Can I Do Now?* Minneapolis: Bethany House, 1990. Helps parents deal with the past and the present.

Notes

Introduction

[1]"New Association for Adult Children Forms," *Changes* (Sept.-Oct. 1990), p. 17.

[2]It is never too early to begin, either, according to recent studies. "One study shows that severely prolonged marital stress during pregnancy can even lead to future delinquency and chronic health problems in the child." Many "prenatal psychologists" are convinced "that the fetus from the age of 6 months is equipped with a kind of emotional radar that enables him to sense and respond to his mother's emotions." Jane Heimlich, "Influencing the Unborn Child," *Cincinnati Enquirer,* May 28, 1986, p. C-4.

Chapter 1: Shame-Bound Parenting: Roots and Fruits

[1]Francis Brown, S. R. Driver and Charles Briggs, *A Hebrew and English Lexicon of the Old Testament* (Oxford: Clarendon Press, 1968), p. 457.

Chapter 2: Choosing Life: Recovering

[1]Steve Lynch, in *The Carleton Voice* (Summer 1985), quoted in Jean Illsey Clarke and Connie Dawson, *Growing Up Again* (Center City, Minn.: Hazelden, 1989), p. 77.

[2]Associated Press, "Study: Depression Impedes Mother-Infant Relationship," *Cincinnati Enquirer,* April 10, 1991, p. D-5.

Chapter 4: Choosing Grace: Releasing

[1]Ellen Walker, *Growing Up with My Children* (Center City, Minn.: Hazelden, 1988), p. v.

[2]Colin Brown, ed., *The New International Dictionary of New Testament Theology,* Vol. II (Grand Rapids: Zondervan, 1986), p. 115.

[3]Colin Brown, ed., *The New International Dictionary of New Testament Theology,* Vol. I (Grand

Rapids: Zondervan, 1986), p. 697.

[4]Robert Enright and Robert Zell, "Problems Encountered When We Forgive One Another," *Journal of Psychology and Christianity* 8 (1989), pp. 52-60.

[5]Gayle Rosellini and Mark Worden, *Taming Your Turbulent Past* (Pompano Beach, Fla.: Health Communications, 1987), p. 179.

Chapter 5: We Can Learn What We Don't Know

[1]Kay Whitmore, "Fourth-Graders Teach Parents a Lesson," *USA Today,* Feb. 1, 1991, p. 9A.

[2]Art Levine, "The Biological Roots of Good Mothering," *U.S. News & World Report,* Feb. 25, 1991, p. 61.

[3]Jack Balswick and Judith Balswick, *The Family: A Christian Perspective on the Contemporary Home* (Grand Rapids: Baker, 1989), p. 103.

[4]The chart in figure 5-1 contains information adapted from pages 116-23 in Jean Illsey Clarke and Connie Dawson's *Growing Up Again.* See appendix C for more about this helpful resource.

[5]Balswick and Balswick, *The Family,* pp. 105-6.

[6]Adapted from Clarke and Dawson, *Growing Up Again,* pp. 58-59.

Chapter 6: We Can Learn and Teach About God

[1]Les Parrott, "A Faith of My Own," *Moody Monthly,* Feb. 1992, p. 22.

[2]I am indebted to my senior pastor, Dr. Ray Dupont, for suggesting this exercise and for other ideas on the relationship between our God-concepts and our parenting.

[3]Sandra D. Wilson, *Counseling Adult Children of Alcoholics,* Resources for Christian Counseling, Vol. 21, ed. Gary Collins (Dallas: Word Books, 1989), pp. 97-98.

[4]Points 1-5 adapted from Shirley Morgenthaler, *Right from the Start* (St. Louis: Concordia, 1989), pp. 90-92.

Chapter 7: We Can Learn to Really Love Our Children

[1]Margery Williams, *The Velveteen Rabbit* (New York: Avon Books, 1975), pp. 5-6.

[2]Archibald Hart, *Feeling Free* (Old Tappan, N.J.: Revell, 1979), p. 126.

[3]This poem by Mitzi Chandler appeared in the July-August 1991 issue of *Changes* magazine.

[4]See Alice and Robert Fryling, *A Handbook for Parents* (Downers Grove, Ill.: InterVarsity Press, 1991), pp. 35-36.

Chapter 8: We Can Learn to Have Realistic Expectations

[1]I read a similar application of the "frog to prince" fairy tale several years ago in *Christian Psychology Today,* a quarterly publication of the Minirth-Meier Clinic in Richardson, Texas. I think the author was Jan Meier.

[2]"Teachers Try Fliers to Stop Child Abuse," *The Washington Post,* rpt. *Cincinnati Enquirer,* Nov. 17, 1990, p. D-4.

[3]Nancy Gibbs, "Murders They Wrote," *Time,* April 1, 1991, p. 29.

Chapter 9: We Can Learn to Talk and Touch

[1]This story appeared in the *Our Daily Bread* devotional for April 2, 1991.

²This is a portion of a poem by Rhonda Gale Pletcher that appeared in *Heartstrings* newsletter (July-Oct. 1991).
³Ibid.
⁴"Love Links, " *Prevention,* Oct. 1991, p. 16.

Chapter 10: We Can Learn to Feel Good About Feelings
¹For examples of Jesus' displaying intense emotion, see Luke 10:21; John 11:35; Matthew 26:38; John 2:14-16.
²Regarding conflict, see Acts 15:37-41 (it is not always harmful) and Romans 12:18 (it is not always avoidable). Regarding anger, see Mark 3:5; John 2:13-17; Ephesians 4:26. Regarding Christians always being happy and "nice," see Romans 12:15; John 11:35; Luke 22:42-44; Matthew 12:38-39. Note that while Christians are not promised constant "happiness," God does offer his abiding peace in the midst of this world's troubles. For example, see John 16:33 and Philippians 4:7.
³Linda Albert, "Parents Must Work to Change Pattern of Hiding Feelings," *Cincinnati Enquirer,* July 5, 1990, p. C-2.
⁴For a more extensive list see Wilson, *Counseling Adult Children of Alcoholics,* p. 145.

Chapter 11: We Can Learn to Like Limits
¹T. Berry Brazelton, "Milestones: How Kids Learn Who They Are," *Family Circle,* Feb.1, 1991, pp. 81-84.
²Leslie R. Kelder et al., "Perceptions of Physical Punishment: The Relation to Childhood and Adolescent Experiences," *Journal of Interpersonal Violence,* 6, no. 4 (Dec 1991), pp. 432-45.
³Proverbs 22:15 describes a child's heart with the word "foolishness." When parents set correcting and disciplining boundaries, Proverbs 9:7-8 tells us to expect anger or even open hostility from our children's foolish hearts.
⁴This quotation and the ideas for managing children in public are taken from "Kids in Public: Guidelines for Getting Your Children to Behave" by John Rosemond, which appeared in *Better Homes and Gardens* (Dec. 1991, p. 34). Dr. Rosemond has written several parenting books, including *Parent Power!* (Kansas City, Mo.: Andrews and McMeel, 1991).
⁵Ellen Goodman, "On the Children's Shoulders," *Family Therapy Networker,* March-April 1985, p. 15. (Italics mine.)
⁶Nancy Day, "I Want to See My Grandchildren: New Rights for Grandparents," *Family Circle,* Nov. 26, 1991, pp. 45-46, 50.

Chapter 12: We Can Learn to Have Fun (If We Work at It!)
¹Quoted in Cecilia Deck, "Workaholism Shows No Signs of Letting Up," *Cincinnati Enquirer,* July 21, 1991, p. H-2.
²Leslie Phillips, "No Holiday for Abuse Victims," *USA Today,* Dec. 12, 1990, p. A-2.
³This point is made by Gary Oliver in "Making Christmas Joyful Again," *Confident Living,* Dec. 1990, pp. 31-32.

Chapter 13: We Can Learn to Give Wings Not Strings
¹See Mark 10:43-45 where Jesus responds to the disciples' inquiries about power

positions with instructions about cultivating a servant spirit.

[2]Jack Balswick and Judith Balswick, "A Maturity-Empowering Model of Christian Parenting," *Journal of Psychology and Theology* 17, no. 1 (1989), pp. 36-43.

[3]William Coleman, *How to Go Home Without Feeling Like a Child* (Dallas: Word Books, 1991), p. 32.

[4]In *Prodigals and Those Who Love Them* (Colorado Springs, Colo.: Focus on the Family, 1991), Ruth Graham shares honest, encouraging words written during the prodigal years of her two sons.

Chapter 14: Life-Giving Legacies
[1]Ellen Walker, *Growing Up with My Children,* p. 141.
[2]Ibid.

Appendix A
[1]This list appeared in the article "Overcoming The Trauma of Incest," in the October 1988 issue of *Virtue* magazine (pp. 18-22). It originally appeared in David Peters's helpful book *A Betrayal of Innocence* (Waco, Tex.: Word Books, 1986). See appendix C for other books on child sexual abuse.

[2]Peters's inclusion of this indicator is highly controversial these days. However, I agree with this indicator's presence on the list.

Every pressure you feel you decide to excel in business venture.

Always throwing me a curve.

The I.R.S. moves in + you do something new + weird with your business that I can't handle alone but feel alone in handling.

Or purchase or spend - perhaps business or program related spending

So I deal with double + triple wammies. No comfort for me at home alone (never) or with others.